OpenStack Essentials

Second Edition

Untangle the complexity of OpenStack clouds through this practical tutorial

Dan Radez

BIRMINGHAM - MUMBAI

OpenStack Essentials

Second Edition

First published: May 2015

Second edition: August 2016

Production reference: 1240816

Published by Packt Publishing Ltd.
Livery Place
35 Livery Street
Birmingham B3 2PB, UK.

ISBN 978-1-78646-266-4

www.packtpub.com

Credits

Author
Dan Radez

Reviewer
Vinoth Kumar Selvaraj

Commissioning Editor
Kartikey Pandey

Acquisition Editor
Divya Poojari

Content Development Editor
Trusha Shriyan

Technical Editor
Nirant Carvalho

Copy Editors
Madhusudan Uchil
Safis Editing

Project Coordinator
Kinjal Bari

Proofreader
Safis Editing

Indexer
Hemangini Bari

Graphics
Kirk D'Penha

Production Coordinator
Shantanu N. Zagade

Cover Work
Shantanu N. Zagade

About the Author

Dan Radez joined the OpenStack community in 2012 in an operator role. His experience is focused on installing, maintaining, and integrating OpenStack clusters. He has been given the opportunity to internationally present OpenStack content to a range of audiences of varying expertise. In January 2015, Dan joined the OPNFV community and has been working to integrate RDO Manager with SDN controllers and the networking features necessary for NFV.

Dan's experience includes web application programming, systems release engineering, and virtualization product development. Most of these roles have had an open source community focus to them. In his spare time, Dan enjoys spending time with his wife and three boys, training for and racing triathlons, and tinkering with electronics projects.

About the Reviewer

Vinoth Kumar Selvaraj works as a DevOps engineer at CD Cloudenablers Pvt Ltd, a cloud technology startup based in Chennai, India.

He has also reviewed *Openstack Cloud Security*. *Learning OpenStack High Availability*, and *Learning OpenStack* (Video), all by *Packt Publishing*.

In his spare time, Vinoth blogs about OpenStack at his website, `http://www.hellovinoth.com`, and shares his thoughts via his Twitter handle, `@vinoth6664`.

I would like to thank my *amma, appa, anna,* and friends for their love and support.

My special thanks to our Cloudenablers team for giving me this opportunity and motivation to explore things.

www.PacktPub.com

eBooks, discount offers, and more

Did you know that Packt offers eBook versions of every book published, with PDF and ePub files available? You can upgrade to the eBook version at www.PacktPub.com and as a print book customer, you are entitled to a discount on the eBook copy. Get in touch with us at customercare@packtpub.com for more details.

At www.PacktPub.com, you can also read a collection of free technical articles, sign up for a range of free newsletters and receive exclusive discounts and offers on Packt books and eBooks.

https://www2.packtpub.com/books/subscription/packtlib

Do you need instant solutions to your IT questions? PacktLib is Packt's online digital book library. Here, you can search, access, and read Packt's entire library of books.

Why subscribe?

- Fully searchable across every book published by Packt
- Copy and paste, print, and bookmark content
- On demand and accessible via a web browser

Table of Contents

Preface

OpenStack is a widely popular cloud-computing platform. Each of the OpenStack components that will be covered in subsequent chapters will be discussed in this preface. This will give you a high-level overview of these components and how they work together.

This book offers step-by-step practical instructions to help you quickly navigate through the complexities of OpenStack. While the examples in this book are situational, it can also be used as a reference for Linux-related topics and commands. This book provides you with the ability to reference both troubleshooting steps and specific commands for resolving complex issues.

What this book covers

Chapter 1, *RDO Installation*, presents a standard installation and an advanced installation of the RDO distribution of OpenStack. A demonstration architecture will be defined, and step-by-step instructions will be given.

Chapter 2, *Identity Management*, talks about Keystone, which is the identity-management component of OpenStack. You will be introduced to basic username-password authentication and the structure of how Keystone manages users, roles, tenants, and services.

Chapter 3, *Image Management* , talks about Glance, which is the image-management component. The process flow of how images are built, added to the registry, and consumed in the cluster will be presented.

Chapter 4, *Network Management*, talks about Neutron, which is the network-management component. Neutron can create and allocate virtual networks, routers, and IP addresses to OpenStack tenants. There is system preparation that is necessary for the cluster to allow external connectivity for instances.

Chapter 5, *Instance Management*, talks about Nova, which is the instance-management component. It is in charge of keeping track of which resources are used on which hypervisors, scheduling new instances for launch, and gathering all the resources necessary for an instance launch.

Chapter 6, *Block Storage*, talks about Cinder, which is the block storage-management component. It creates volumes and presents them to the instances. This can be done with multiple storage engines.

Chapter 7, *Object Storage*, talks about Swift, which is the object storage-management component. It creates object containers and manages file objects in the containers. Swift can optionally be backed with storage engines other than the default Swift object storage engine.

Chapter 8, *Telemetry*, talks about Ceilometer, which is the telemetry and metering component. It monitors the cluster and collects statistics of the resources that are in use.

Chapter 9, *Orchestration*, talks about Heat, which is the orchestration component. It is able to launch multiple instances and coordinate exchanging information about the instances within a heat stack.

Chapter 10, *Docker*, talks about containerization, which has become a prominent part of cloud computing. I'll go through the steps it takes to convert a compute node to a compute node that can support Docker containers.

Chapter 11, *Scaling Horizontally*, tells you how add a compute node and configure HAProxy by simply installing a new node, telling it where the control services are, and starting compute services.

Chapter 12, *Monitoring*, shows you how to use Nagios to perform basic monitoring.

Chapter 13, *Troubleshooting*, discusses some of the common issues that will surface while running an OpenStack cluster and where to go to find out where the error messages have been recorded.

What you need for this book

While this book can be used by itself, you can benefit greatly by having a system with Red Hat Enterprise Linux available. The commands and resources discussed in this book are best learned when you have the ability to execute them on a test system. It is highly recommended you use Liberty software.

Who this book is for

This book is perfect for administrators, cloud engineers, and operators who want to get started with OpenStack, solve basic problems encountered during deployment, and get up to speed with the latest release of OpenStack. Familiarity with the Linux command line and experience with Linux system administration is expected.

Conventions

In this book, you will find a number of text styles that distinguish between different kinds of information. Here are some examples of these styles and an explanation of their meaning.

Code words in text, database table names, folder names, filenames, file extensions, pathnames, dummy URLs, user input, and Twitter handles are shown as follows: " In addition to the client package, you will also need the overcloudrc file from the undercloud."

A block of code is set as follows:

```
define service {
check_command check_nrpe!check_ovs_tunnel
host_name compute
service_description OVS tunnel connectivity
use generic-service
}
```

Any command-line input or output is written as follows:

```
myhost# sudo ip addr add 192.0.2.222/24 dev bridget
myhost# sudo ip link set up dev bridget
```

New terms and **important words** are shown in bold. Words that you see on the screen, for example, in menus or dialog boxes, appear in the text like this: "Click on **Create User**, and you're ready to start using the user's login and the new project."

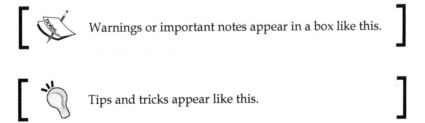

[Warnings or important notes appear in a box like this.]

[Tips and tricks appear like this.]

Reader feedback

Feedback from our readers is always welcome. Let us know what you think about this book—what you liked or disliked. Reader feedback is important for us as it helps us develop titles that you will really get the most out of.

To send us general feedback, simply e-mail `feedback@packtpub.com`, and mention the book's title in the subject of your message.

If there is a topic that you have expertise in and you are interested in either writing or contributing to a book, see our author guide at `www.packtpub.com/authors`.

Customer support

Now that you are the proud owner of a Packt book, we have a number of things to help you to get the most from your purchase.

Errata

Although we have taken every care to ensure the accuracy of our content, mistakes do happen. If you find a mistake in one of our books—maybe a mistake in the text or the code—we would be grateful if you could report this to us. By doing so, you can save other readers from frustration and help us improve subsequent versions of this book. If you find any errata, please report them by visiting `http://www.packtpub.com/submit-errata`, selecting your book, clicking on the **Errata Submission Form** link, and entering the details of your errata. Once your errata are verified, your submission will be accepted and the errata will be uploaded to our website or added to any list of existing errata under the Errata section of that title.

To view the previously submitted errata, go to `https://www.packtpub.com/books/content/support` and enter the name of the book in the search field. The required information will appear under the **Errata** section.

Piracy

Piracy of copyrighted material on the Internet is an ongoing problem across all media. At Packt, we take the protection of our copyright and licenses very seriously. If you come across any illegal copies of our works in any form on the Internet, please provide us with the location address or website name immediately so that we can pursue a remedy.

Please contact us at copyright@packtpub.com with a link to the suspected pirated material.

We appreciate your help in protecting our authors and our ability to bring you valuable content.

Questions

If you have a problem with any aspect of this book, you can contact us at questions@packtpub.com, and we will do our best to address the problem.

1
RDO Installation

OpenStack has a very modular design, and because of this design, there are lots of moving parts. It is overwhelming to start walking through installing and using OpenStack without understanding the internal architecture of the components that make up OpenStack. In this chapter, we'll look at these components. Each component in OpenStack manages a different resource that can be virtualized for the end user. Separating the management of each of the types of resources that can be virtualized into separate components makes the OpenStack architecture very modular. If a particular service or resource provided by a component is not required, then the component is optional to an OpenStack deployment. Once the components that make up OpenStack have been covered, we will discuss the configuration of a community-supported distribution of OpenStack called RDO.

OpenStack architecture

Let's start by outlining some simple categories to group these services into. Logically, the components of OpenStack are divided into three groups:

- Control
- Network
- Compute

The control tier runs the **Application Programming Interface** (API) services, web interface, database, and message bus. The network tier runs network service agents for networking, and the compute tier is the virtualization hypervisor. It has services and agents to handle virtual machines. All of the components use a database and/or a message bus. The database can be MySQL, MariaDB, or PostgreSQL. The most popular message buses are RabbitMQ, Qpid, and ActiveMQ. For smaller deployments, the database and messaging services usually run on the control node, but they could have their own nodes if required.

In a simple multi-node deployment, the control and networking services are installed on one server and the compute services are installed onto another server. OpenStack could be installed on one node or more than two nodes, but a good baseline for being able to scale out later is to put control and network together and compute by itself. An OpenStack cluster can scale far beyond a few nodes, and we will look at scaling beyond this basic deployment in *Chapter 11, Scaling Horizontally*.

Now that a base logical architecture of OpenStack has been defined, let's look at what components make up this basic architecture. To do that, we'll first touch on the web interface and then work toward collecting the resources necessary to launch an instance. Finally, we will look at what components are available to add resources to a launched instance.

Dashboard

The OpenStack dashboard is the web interface component provided with OpenStack. You'll sometimes hear the terms dashboard and **Horizon** used interchangeably. Technically, they are not the same thing. This book will refer to the web interface as the dashboard. The team that develops the web interface maintains both the dashboard interface and the Horizon framework that the dashboard uses.

More important than getting these terms right is understanding the commitment that the team that maintains this code base has made to the OpenStack project. They have pledged to include support for all the officially accepted components that are included in OpenStack. Visit the OpenStack website (`http://www.openstack.org/`) to get an official list of OpenStack components.

The dashboard cannot do anything that the API cannot do. All the actions that are taken through the dashboard result in calls to the API to complete the task requested by the end user. Throughout this book, we will examine how to use the web interface and the API clients to execute tasks in an OpenStack cluster. Next, we will discuss both the dashboard and the underlying components that the dashboard makes calls to when creating OpenStack resources.

Keystone

Keystone is the identity management component. The first thing that needs to happen while connecting to an OpenStack deployment is authentication. In its most basic installation, Keystone will manage tenants, users, and roles and be a catalog of services and endpoints for all the components in the running cluster.

Everything in OpenStack must exist in a tenant. A tenant is simply a grouping of objects. Users, instances, and networks are examples of objects. They cannot exist outside of a tenant. Another name for a tenant is a project. On the command line, the term tenant is used. In the web interface, the term project is used.

Users must be granted a role in a tenant. It's important to understand this relationship between the user and a tenant via a role. In *Chapter 2*, *Identity Management*, we will look at how to create the user and tenant and how to associate the user with a role in a tenant. For now, understand that a user cannot log in to the cluster unless they are a member of a tenant. Even the administrator has a tenant. Even the users the OpenStack components use to communicate with each other have to be members of a tenant to be able to authenticate.

Keystone also keeps a catalog of services and endpoints of each of the OpenStack components in the cluster. This is advantageous because all of the components have different API endpoints. By registering them all with Keystone, an end user only needs to know the address of the Keystone server to interact with the cluster. When a call is made to connect to a component other than Keystone, the call will first have to be authenticated, so Keystone will be contacted regardless.

Within the communication to Keystone, the client also asks Keystone for the address of the component the user intended to connect to. This makes managing the endpoints easier. If all the endpoints were distributed to the end users, then it would be a complex process to distribute a change in one of the endpoints to all of the end users. By keeping the catalog of services and endpoints in Keystone, a change is easily distributed to end users as new requests are made to connect to the components.

By default, Keystone uses username/password authentication to request a token and the acquired tokens for subsequent requests. All the components in the cluster can use the token to verify the user and the user's access. Keystone can also be integrated into other common authentication systems instead of relying on the username and password authentication provided by Keystone. In *Chapter 2*, *Identity Management*, each of these resources will be explored. We'll walk through creating a user and a tenant and look at the service catalog.

Glance

Glance is the image management component. Once we're authenticated, there are a few resources that need to be available for an instance to launch. The first resource we'll look at is the disk image to launch from. Before a server is useful, it needs to have an operating system installed on it. This is a boilerplate task that cloud computing has streamlined by creating a registry of pre-installed disk images to boot from. Glance serves as this registry within an OpenStack deployment. In preparation for an instance to launch, a copy of a selected Glance image is first cached to the compute node where the instance is being launched. Then, a copy is made to the ephemeral disk location of the new instance. Subsequent instances launched on the same compute node using the same disk image will use the cached copy of the Glance image.

The images stored in Glance are sometimes called sealed-disk images. These images are disk images that have had the operating system installed but have had things such as the **Secure Shell** (**SSH**) host key and network device MAC addresses removed. This makes the disk images generic, so they can be reused and launched repeatedly without the running copies conflicting with each other. To do this, the host-specific information is provided or generated at boot. The provided information is passed in through a post-boot configuration facility called **cloud-init**.

Usually, these images are downloaded from distribution's download pages. If you search the Internet for your favorite distribution's name and cloud image, you will probably get a link to where to download a generic pre-built copy of a Glance image, also known as a cloud image.

The images can also be customized for special purposes beyond a base operating system installation. If there was a specific purpose for which an instance would be launched many times, then some of the repetitive configuration tasks could be performed ahead of time and built into the disk image. For example, if a disk image was intended to be used to build a cluster of web servers, it would make sense to install a web server package on the disk image before it was used to launch an instance. It would save time and bandwidth to do it once before it is registered with Glance instead of doing this package installation and configuration over and over each time a web server instance is booted.

There are quite a few ways to build these disk images. The simplest way is to do a virtual machine installation manually, make sure that the host-specific information is removed, and include cloud-init in the built image. Cloud-init is packaged in most major distributions; you should be able to simply add it to a package list. There are also tools to make this happen in a more autonomous fashion. Some of the more popular tools are **virt-install**, **Oz**, and **appliance-creator**. The most important thing about building a cloud image for OpenStack is to make sure that cloud-init is installed. Cloud-init is a script that should run post boot to connect back to the metadata service.

In *Chapter 3*, *Image Management*, when Glance is covered in greater detail, we will download a pre-built image and use it to demonstrate how Glance works.

Neutron

Neutron is the network management component. With Keystone, we're authenticated, and from Glance, a disk image will be provided. The next resource required for launch is a virtual network. Neutron is an API frontend (and a set of agents) that manages the **Software Defined Networking** (**SDN**) infrastructure for you. When an OpenStack deployment is using Neutron, it means that each of your tenants can create virtual isolated networks. Each of these isolated networks can be connected to virtual routers to create routes between the virtual networks. A virtual router can have an external gateway connected to it, and external access can be given to each instance by associating a floating IP on an external network with an instance. Neutron then puts all the configuration in place to route the traffic sent to the floating IP address through these virtual network resources into a launched instance. This is also called **Networking as a Service** (**NaaS**). NaaS is the capability to provide networks and network resources on demand via software.

By default, the OpenStack distribution we will install uses **Open vSwitch** to orchestrate the underlying virtualized networking infrastructure. Open vSwitch is a virtual managed switch. As long as the nodes in your cluster have simple connectivity to each other, Open vSwitch can be the infrastructure configured to isolate the virtual networks for the tenants in OpenStack. There are also many vendor plugins that would allow you to replace Open vSwitch with a physical managed switch to handle the virtual networks. Neutron even has the capability to use multiple plugins to manage multiple network appliances. As an example, Open vSwitch and a vendor's appliance could be used in parallel to manage virtual networks in an OpenStack deployment. This is a great example of how OpenStack is built to provide flexibility and choice to its users.

Networking is the most complex component of OpenStack to configure and maintain. This is because Neutron is built around core networking concepts. To successfully deploy Neutron, you need to understand these core concepts and how they interact with one another. In *Chapter 4, Network Management*, we'll spend time covering these concepts while building the Neutron infrastructure for an OpenStack deployment.

Nova

Nova is the instance management component. An authenticated user who has access to a Glance image and has created a network for an instance to live on is almost ready to tie all of this together and launch an instance. The last resources that are required are a key pair and a security group. A key pair is simply an SSH key pair. OpenStack will allow you to import your own key pair or generate one to use. When the instance is launched, the public key is placed in the authorized_keys file so that a password-less SSH connection can be made to the running instance.

Before that SSH connection can be made, the security groups have to be opened to allow the connection to be made. A security group is a firewall at the cloud infrastructure layer. The OpenStack distribution we'll use will have a default security group with rules to allow instances to communicate with each other within the same security group, but rules will have to be added for **Internet Control Message Protocol (ICMP)**, SSH, and other connections to be made from outside the security group.

Once there's an image, network, key pair, and security group available, an instance can be launched. The resource's identifiers are provided to Nova, and Nova looks at what resources are being used on which hypervisors, and schedules the instance to spawn on a compute node. The compute node gets the Glance image, creates the virtual network devices, and boots the instance. During the boot, cloud-init should run and connect to the metadata service. The metadata service provides the SSH public key needed for SSH login to the instance and, if provided, any post-boot configuration that needs to happen. This could be anything from a simple shell script to an invocation of a configuration management engine.

In *Chapter 5, Instance Management*, we'll walk through each of the pieces of Nova and see how to configure them so that instances can be launched and communicated with.

Cinder

Cinder is the block storage management component. Volumes can be created and attached to instances. Then they are used on the instances as any other block device would be used. On the instance, the block device can be partitioned and a filesystem can be created and mounted. Cinder also handles snapshots. Snapshots can be taken of the block volumes or of instances. Instances can also use these snapshots as a boot source.

There is an extensive collection of storage backends that can be configured as the backing store for Cinder volumes and snapshots. By default, **Logical Volume Manager (LVM)** is configured. GlusterFS and Ceph are two popular software-based storage solutions. There are also many plugins for hardware appliances.

In *Chapter 6, Block Storage*, we'll take a look at creating and attaching volumes to instances, taking snapshots, and configuring additional storage backends to Cinder.

Swift

Swift is the object storage management component. Object storage is a simple content-only storage system. Files are stored without the metadata that a block filesystem has. These are simply containers and files. The files are simply content. Swift has two layers as part of its deployment: the proxy and the storage engine. The proxy is the API layer. It's the service that the end user communicates with. The proxy is configured to talk to the storage engine on the user's behalf. By default, the storage engine is the Swift storage engine. It's able to do software-based storage distribution and replication. GlusterFS and Ceph are also popular storage backends for Swift. They have similar distribution and replication capabilities to those of Swift storage.

In *Chapter 7, Object Storage*, we'll work with object content and the configuration involved in setting up an alternative storage backend for Swift.

Ceilometer

Ceilometer is the telemetry component. It collects resource measurements and is able to monitor the cluster. Ceilometer was originally designed as a metering system for billing users. As it was being built, there was a realization that it would be useful for more than just billing and turned into a general-purpose telemetry system.

Ceilometer meters measure the resources being used in an OpenStack deployment. When Ceilometer reads a meter, it's called a sample. These **samples** get recorded on a regular basis. A collection of samples is called a statistic. Telemetry **statistics** will give insights into how the resources of an OpenStack deployment are being used.

The samples can also be used for alarms. Alarms are nothing but monitors that watch for a certain criterion to be met. These alarms were originally designed for Heat autoscaling. We'll look more at getting statistics and setting alarms in *Chapter 8, Telemetry*. Let's finish listing out OpenStack components by talking about Heat.

Heat

Heat is the orchestration component. Orchestration is the process of launching multiple instances that are intended to work together. In orchestration, there is a file, known as a **template**, used to define what will be launched. In this template, there can also be ordering or dependencies set up between the instances. Data that needs to be passed between the instances for configuration can also be defined in these templates. Heat is also compatible with AWS CloudFormation templates and implements additional features in addition to the AWS CloudFormation template language.

To use Heat, one of these templates is written to define a set of instances that needs to be launched. When a template launches, it creates a collection of virtual resources (instances, networks, storage devices, and so on); this collection of resources is called a **stack**. When a stack is spawned, the ordering and dependencies, shared configuration data, and post-boot configuration are coordinated via Heat.

Heat is not configuration management. It is orchestration. It is intended to coordinate launching the instances, passing configuration data, and executing simple post-boot configuration. A very common post-boot configuration task is invoking an actual configuration management engine to execute more complex post-boot configuration. In *Chapter 9, Orchestration*, we'll explore creating a Heat template and launching a stack using Heat.

OpenStack installation

The list of components that have been covered is not the full list. This is just a small subset to get you started with using and understanding OpenStack. Further components that are defaults in an OpenStack installation provide many advanced capabilities that we will not be able to cover. Now that we have introduced the OpenStack components, we will illustrate how they work together as a running OpenStack installation. To illustrate an OpenStack installation, we first need to install one. Let's use the RDO Project's OpenStack distribution to do that. RDO has two installation methods; we will discuss both of them and focus on one of them throughout this book.

Manual installation and configuration of OpenStack involves installing, configuring, and registering each of the components we covered in the previous chapter, and also multiple databases and a messaging system. It's a very involved, repetitive, error-prone, and sometimes confusing process. Fortunately, there are a few distributions that include tools to automate this installation and configuration process.

One such distribution is the RDO Project distribution. RDO, as a name, doesn't officially mean anything. It is just the name of a community-supported distribution of OpenStack. The RDO Project takes the upstream OpenStack code, packages it in RPMs and provides documentation, forums, IRC channels, and other resources for the RDO community to use and support each other in running OpenStack on RPM-based systems. There are no modifications to the upstream OpenStack code in the RDO distribution. The RDO project packages the code that is in each of the upstream releases of OpenStack. This means that we'll use an open source, community-supported distribution of vanilla OpenStack for our example installation. RDO should be able to be run on any RPM-based system. We will now look at the two installation tools that are part of the RDO Project, Packstack and RDO Triple-O. We will focus on using RDO Triple-O in this book. The RDO Project recommends RDO Triple-O for installations that intend to deploy a more feature-rich environment. One example is High Availability. RDO Triple-O is able to do HA deployments and Packstack is not. There is still great value in doing an installation with Packstack. Packstack is intended to give you a very lightweight, quick way to stand up a basic OpenStack installation. Let's start by taking a quick look at Packstack so you are familiar with how quick and lightweight is it.

Installing RDO using Packstack

Packstack is an installation tool for OpenStack intended for demonstration and proof-of-concept deployments. Packstack uses SSH to connect to each of the nodes and invokes a puppet run (specifically, a puppet apply) on each of the nodes to install and configure OpenStack.

> RDO website: `http://openstack.redhat.com`
>
> Packstack installation: `http://openstack.redhat.com/install/quickstart`

The RDO Project quick start gives instructions to install RDO using Packstack in three simple steps:

1. Update the system and install the RDO release `rpm` as follows:

   ```
   sudo yum update -y
   sudo yum install -y http://rdo.fedorapeople.org/rdo-release.rpm
   ```

2. Install Packstack as shown in the following command:

   ```
   sudo yum install -y openstack-packstack
   ```

3. Run Packstack as shown in the following command:

   ```
   sudo packstack --allinone
   ```

The all-in-one installation method works well to run on a virtual machine as your all-in-one OpenStack node. In reality, however, a cluster will usually use more than one node beyond a simple learning environment. Packstack is capable of doing multinode installations, though you will have to read the RDO Project documentation for Packstack on the RDO Project wiki. We will not go any deeper with Packstack than the all-in-one installation we have just walked through.

> Don't avoid doing an all-in-one installation; it really is as simple as the steps make it out to be, and there is value in getting an OpenStack installation up and running quickly.

Installing RDO using Triple-O

The Triple-O project is an OpenStack installation tool developed by the OpenStack community. A Triple-O deployment consists of two OpenStack deployments. One of the deployments is an all-in-one OpenStack installation that is used as a provisioning tool to deploy a multi-node target OpenStack deployment. This target deployment is the deployment intended for end users. Triple-O stands for OpenStack on OpenStack. OpenStack on OpenStack would be OOO, which lovingly became referred to as Triple-O. It may sound like madness to use OpenStack to deploy OpenStack, but consider that OpenStack is really good at provisioning virtual instances. Triple-O applies this strength to bare-metal deployments to deploy a target OpenStack environment. In Triple-O, the two OpenStacks are called the **undercloud** and the **overcloud**. The undercloud is a baremetal management enabled all-in-one OpenStack installation that will build for you in a very prescriptive way. Baremetal management enabled means it is intended to manage physical machines instead of virtual machines. The overcloud is the target deployment of OpenStack that is intended be exposed to end users. The undercloud will take a cluster of nodes provided to it and deploy the overcloud to them, a fully featured OpenStack deployment. In real deployments, this is done with a collection of baremetal nodes. Fortunately, for learning purposes, we can mock having a bunch of baremetal nodes by using virtual machines.

Mind blown yet? Let's get started with this RDO Manager based OpenStack installation to start unraveling what all this means. There is an RDO Manager quickstart project that we will use to get going.

The RDO Triple-O wiki page will be the most up-to-date place to get started with RDO Triple-O. If you have trouble with the directions in this book, please refer to the wiki. OpenSource changes rapidly and RDO Triple-O is no exception. In particular, note that the directions refer to the Mitaka release of OpenStack. The name of the release will most likely be the first thing that changes on the wiki page that will impact your future deployments with RDO Triple-O.

Start by downloading the pre-built undercloud image from the RDO Project's repositories. This is something you could build yourself but it would take much more time and effort to build than it would take to download the pre-built one. As mentioned earlier, the undercloud is a pretty prescriptive all-in-one deployment which lends itself well to starting with a pre-built image. These instructions come from the readme of the Triple-O quickstart GitHub repository (`https://github.com/redhat-openstack/tripleo-quickstart/`):

```
myhost# mkdir -p /usr/share/quickstart_images/
myhost# cd /usr/share/quickstart_images/
myhost# wget https://ci.centos.org/artifacts/rdo/images/mitaka/delorean/stable/undercloud.qcow2.md5 \
https://ci.centos.org/artifacts/rdo/images/mitaka/delorean/stable/undercloud.qcow2
```

Make sure that your `ssh` key exists:

```
Myhost# ls ~/.ssh
```

If you don't see the `id_rsa` and `id_rsa.pub` files in that directory list, run the command `ssh-keygen`. Then make sure that your public key is in the authorized keys file:

```
myhost# cat ~/.ssh/id_rsa.pub >> ~/.ssh/authorized_keys
```

Once you have the undercloud image and you `ssh` keys pull a copy of the `quickstart.sh` file, install the dependencies and execute the quickstart script:

```
myhost# cd ~
myhost# wget https://raw.githubusercontent.com/redhat-openstack/tripleo-quickstart/master/quickstart.sh
myhost#sh quickstart.sh -u \
file:///usr/share/quickstart_images/undercloud.qcow2 \
localhost
```

`quickstart.sh` will use Ansible to set up the undercloud virtual machine and will define a few extra virtual machines that will be used to mock a collection of baremetal nodes for an overcloud deployment. To see the list of virtual machines that `quickstack.sh` created, use `virsh` to list them:

```
myhost# virsh list --all
 Id    Name                          State
 ----------------------------------------------------------

 17    undercloud                    running
 -        ceph_0                         shut off
 -        compute_0                  shut off
 -        control_0                      shut off
 -        control_1                      shut off
 -        control_2                      shut off
```

Along with the undercloud virtual machine, there are `ceph`, `compute`, and `control` virtual machine definitions. These are the nodes that will be used to deploy the OpenStack overcloud. Using virtual machines like this to deploy OpenStack is not suitable for anything but your own personal OpenStack enrichment. These virtual machines represent physical machines that would be used in a real deployment that would be exposed to end users. To continue the undercloud installation, connect to the undercloud virtual machine and run the undercloud configuration:

```
myhost# ssh -F /root/.quickstart/ssh.config.ansible undercloud
undercloud# openstack undercloud install
```

The undercloud install command will set up the undercloud machine as an all-in-one OpenStack installation ready be told how to deploy the overcloud. Once the undercloud installation is completed, the final steps are to seed the undercloud with configuration about the overcloud deployment and execute the overcloud deployment:

```
undercloud# source stackrc
undercloud# openstack overcloud image upload
undercloud# openstack baremetal import --json instackenv.json
undercloud# openstack baremetal configure boot
undercloud# neutron subnet-list
undercloud# neutron subnet-update <subnet-uuid> --dns-nameserver 8.8.8.8
```

There are also some scripts and other automated ways to make these steps happen: look at the output of the quickstart script or Triple-O quickstart docs in the GitHub repository to get more information about how to automate some of these steps.

The source command puts information into the shell environment to tell the subsequent commands how to communicate with the undercloud. We will look at this more in depth in *Chapter 2, Identity Management*. The image upload command uploads disk images into Glance that will be used to provision the overcloud nodes. We will look at this more in *Chapter 3, Image Management*. The first baremetal command imports information about the overcloud environment that will be deployed. This information was written to the instackenv.json file when the undercloud virtual machine was created by quickstart.sh. The second configures the images that were just uploaded in preparation for provisioning the overcloud nodes. The two neutron commands configure a DNS server for the network that the overclouds will use, in this case Google's. Finally, execute the overcloud deploy:

```
undercloud# openstack overcloud deploy --control-scale 1 --compute-scale
1 --templates --libvirt-type qemu --ceph-storage-scale 1 -e /usr/share/
openstack-tripleo-heat-templates/environments/storage-environment.yaml
```

Let's talk about what this command is doing. In OpenStack, there are two basic node types, control and compute. A control node runs the OpenStack API services, OpenStack scheduling service, database services, and messaging services. Pretty much everything except the hypervisors are part of the control tier and are segregated onto control nodes in a basic deployment. In an HA deployment, there are at least three control nodes. This is why you see three control nodes in the list of virtual machines quickstart.sh created. RDO Triple-O can do HA deployments, though we will focus on non-HA deployments in this book. Note that in the command you have just executed, control scale and compute scale are both set to 1. This means that you are deploying one control and one compute node. The other virtual machines will not be used. Take note of the libvirt-type parameter. It is only required if the compute node itself it virtualized, which is what we are doing with RDO Triple-O, to set the configuration properly for the instances to nested. Nested virtualization is when virtual machines are running inside of a virtual machine. In this case, the instances will be virtual machines running inside of the compute node, which is a virtual machine. Finally, the ceph storage scale and storage environment file will deploy Ceph at the storage backend for Glance and Cinder. If you leave off the Ceph and storage environment file parameters, one less virtual machine will be used for deployment. There is more information on storage backends in *Chapter 6, Block Storage*. The indication the overcloud deploy has succeeded will give you a Keystone endpoint and a success message:

```
Overcloud Endpoint: http://192.0.2.6:5000/v2.0

Overcloud Deployed
```

Connecting to your Overcloud

Finally, before we dig into looking at the OpenStack components that have been installed and configured, let's identify three ways that you can connect to the freshly installed overcloud deployment:

- **From the undercloud**: This is the quickest way to access the overcloud. When the overcloud deployment completed, a file named overcloudrc was created. In *Chapter 2, Identity Management*, we will investigate this file in more detail. Throughout the rest of the book, this method will be used.

- **Install the client libraries**: Both RDO Triple-O and Packstack were installed from the RDO release repository. By installing this release repository, in the same way that was demonstrated earlier for Packstack on another computer, the OpenStack client libraries can be installed on that computer. If these libraries are installed on a computer that can route the network the overcloud was installed on then the overcloud can be accessed from that computer the same as it can from the undercloud. This is helpful if you do not want to be tied to jumping through the undercloud node to access the overcloud:

```
laptop# sudo yum install -y http://rdo.fedorapeople.org/rdo-release.rpm

laptop# sudo yum install python-openstackclient
```

In addition to the client package, you will also need the overcloudrc file from the undercloud.

As an example, you can install the packages on the host machine you have just run quickstart.sh and make the overcloud routable by adding an IP address to the OVS bridge the virtual machines were attached to:

```
myhost# sudo ip addr add 192.0.2.222/24 dev bridget

myhost# sudo ip link set up dev bridget
```

Once this is done, the commands in the subsequent chapters could be run from the host machine instead of the undercloud virtual machine.

- **The OpenStack dashboard**: OpenStack's included web interface is called the **dashboard**. Each chapter in this book will conclude by walking through how to complete the same action from the command-line interface with the web interface, if the functionality exists. In the installation you have just completed, you can access the overcloud's dashboard by first running the two `ip` commands used in the second of the preceding commands, then connecting to the IP address indicated as the overcloud endpoint but on port `80` instead of `5000`:

`http://192.0.2.6/.`

Summary

After looking at the components that make up an OpenStack installation, we used RDO Triple-O as a provisioning tool. We now have OpenStack installed and running. Now that OpenStack is installed and running, let's walk through each of the components discussed to learn how to use each of them.

In the next chapter, you will take a look at Keystone to manage users, tenants, and roles used in managing identities within the OpenStack cluster.

2
Identity Management

In the previous chapter, we installed OpenStack using RDO Triple-O. Now that OpenStack is ready for use, we will begin to investigate what was installed and how to use it component by component, starting with identity management. Keystone is the identity management component in OpenStack. In this chapter, we will look at service registration and the relationship of users with tenants, and the role of a user in a tenant.

Services and endpoints

Each one of the components in an OpenStack cluster is registered with Keystone. Each of the services has endpoints and each of the services has a user. A service in Keystone is a record of an OpenStack component that will need to be contacted to manage the virtual resources being managed by OpenStack. Endpoints are the URLs to contact these services. Let's look at this on the command line. Remember the overcloudrc file on the instack node? You'll need the information in that file to authenticate and interact with the OpenStack overcloud. The information is as follows:

```
undercloud# cat overcloudrc
export OS_NO_CACHE=True
export OS_CLOUDNAME=overcloud
export OS_AUTH_URL=http://192.0.2.6:5000/v2.0
export NOVA_VERSION=1.1
export COMPUTE_API_VERSION=1.1
export OS_USERNAME=admin
export no_proxy=,192.0.2.6
```

```
export OS_PASSWORD=mg4xQF4bnETuNgGGtp6t9CXMJ
```

```
export PYTHONWARNINGS="ignore:Certificate has no, ignore:A true
SSLContext object is not available"
```

```
export OS_TENANT_NAME=admin
```

Use the information from the overcloudrc file to run this command:

```
control# openstack --os-username admin --os-tenant-name admin \
--os-password mg4xQF4bnETuNgGGtp6t9CXMJ --os-auth-url \
http://192.0.2.6:5000/v2.0/ service list
```

Manually entering Keystone arguments is a real challenge and prone to error. The overcloudrc file thus becomes much more than just a storage place for the user's credentials. If you source the file, then those values are placed in the shell's environment. OpenStack's Python clients know to look at the shell's environment to get these values when they aren't passed as arguments. For example, execute the service-list command again with the overcloudrc file sourced, as follows:

```
undercloud# source overcloudrc
```

```
undercloud# openstack service list
```

As you will see, it is much more manageable to issue this command and subsequent commands now. This list shows all the components that are registered with this OpenStack cluster. Now list the endpoints as follows:

```
control# openstack endpoint list
```

Each service has an endpoint record. Execute an endpoint show on one of the endpoints, as follows:

```
undercloud# openstack endpoint show cd94e1a6830e4110ba96217dc9177632
```

Each of the endpoint records has a public, private, and admin endpoint URL. Public is used for end user communication and the private and admin are used for internal communication between OpenStack components. An end user or a component within the cluster can always ask Keystone for the endpoint of a component, or service, to connect to. This makes it manageable to update the endpoints and be certain that new clients are connecting to the correct endpoints. The only endpoint that needs to be known ahead of time is the Keystone endpoint. Registration of a service and a set of endpoints only allows us to know about a service and how to connect to it. Each of these services also has a user. The services' users are used for inter-component communication. Each of the services authenticates with Keystone to communicate with each other.

Hierarchy of users, projects, and roles

A user is granted a role in a project. A project is simply a grouping of resources. A user can have a role in multiple projects. Without a role in a project, a user cannot create virtual resources in an OpenStack cluster. A user is useless without a role in a project. All virtual resources created in OpenStack must exist in a project. Virtual resources are the virtual infrastructure that OpenStack manages. Among others, instances, networks, storage, and disk images must exist in a project. Recall the services that were just introduced; they all have a user that has a role in a project. If you list the users and projects in your OpenStack installation, you will see a user for each of the components installed in the installed cluster. Then, list one of the user's roles in the service project. Let's use Nova as an example; here's the output summary after you hit the following commands:

```
undercloud# openstack user list
undercloud# openstack project list
undercloud# openstack user role list --project service nova
```

```
+----------------+------------+---------------------+--------------+
|       id       |    name    |       Project       |     User     |
+----------------+------------+---------------------+--------------+
|   {role_id}    |  _member_  |    service          |    nova      |
|   {role_id}    |  admin     |       service       |    nova      |
+----------------+------------+---------------------+--------------+
```

There should not be any need for you to interact with these service users, though there are conventions that are used for creating users for you and end users to interact with the cluster. First, there are only two roles that are currently used, admin and member. administrative and non-administrative privileges respectively. Recall that when we authenticated the admin user earlier, the admin user was authenticating to a project named the same as the username. A common convention for creating project names is to use the same name as that of the user that will be using it unless it is used by a group. If there are multiple users that have roles in a project, a more descriptive name is used for the project's name. Take the admin and service projects as examples of using the user's name or a more descriptive name. There are multiple users in the service project. It is a project for all the users of services. There is only one user that uses the admin tenant – the admin user. Each user that will use an OpenStack deployment will need a user to log in and a project to operate out of. Each user can have a different role in different projects. Let's walk through creating a user and project and giving that user a role in the project.

Creating a user

We will start by creating a user. There are a handful of subcommands for user management. Run the `openstack help` subcommand on user and look through the list of subcommands available. To create a user, use the `user-create` subcommand as follows:

```
undercloud# openstack help user
undercloud# openstack user create danradez
```

A user now exists that has my first and last name as its username. There are other properties that can be set when a user is created. Use `help` in the command-line client to get more information about these properties, as follows:

```
undercloud# openstack help user create
```

All of OpenStack's command-line commands use this syntax convention to display help. You can use the subcommand `help` and pass it the subcommand name that you want help on, and a list of arguments and their descriptions will be displayed. An e-mail or a password could have been set when the user was created. All these properties can also be updated using the `user set` subcommand. Let's update the new user's e-mail as an example:

```
undercloud# openstack user set --email danradez@example.com danradez
```

Here, the new user has been updated to have an e-mail address. Next, set a password for the new user, as follows:

```
undercloud# openstack user set --password supersecret danradez
```

Creating a project

Now that we have a user, we need a project for the user to store its virtual resources. Similar to the subcommands for user management, you can get help on all the subcommands for project management with OpenStack's `help` subcommand. The following `project create` subcommand will create a new project for the new user:

```
undercloud# openstack project create danradez
```

In this example, the project is created using the convention mentioned earlier, with the username as the name of the project. A project also has a description property; use `openstack help project create` or `keystone help project set` to get the syntax to set the project's description.

Make a note that, on the command line, projects have historically been called tenants. If you see references to tenants while you are working with OpenStack, or even in this book, know that a project and a tenant are analogous.

Granting a role

Now that we have a user and a project, they need to be associated with each other with a role. To do this, the user, the project, and a role need to be passed to the `role add` subcommand. Before this is executed, you can use the `role list` command to get a list of roles, as shown in the following code:

```
undercloud# openstack role list
undercloud# openstack user role add --user danradez --project danradez
_member_
```

This command associates the user, the project, and the role with each other. This association can now be displayed using the `user role list` subcommand used earlier, as follows:

```
undercloud# openstack user role list --project danradez danradez
```

That command will show you that the new user was granted the member role in the new project. Now that we have a new user that has a role in a project, we can use this user's password to make command-line API calls in the same way as was done with the admin user.

Logging in with the new user

The easiest way to start using the new user is to make a copy of an existing `overcloudrc` file, update the values in it, and source the file. We conveniently already have an existing `overcloudrc` file that was used for the admin user. Make a copy of it and edit it so that its contents have values respective to your new user, as follows:

```
undercloud# cp overcloudrc overcloudrc_danradez
```

Here are the contents of the new file:

```
export OS_USERNAME=danradez
export OS_TENANT_NAME=danradez
export OS_PASSWORD=supersecret
export OS_AUTH_URL=http://192.0.2.6:5000/v2.0/
```

AUTH_URL here is pointing to the internal URL; the public URL is also a fine choice for this value. You can leave the other values that were in the overcloudrc file in there if you want.

> Remember to use Keystone's service list and endpoint list commands if you want to use a different Keystone endpoint. Next, we must source the new keystonerc file. A simple authentication verification is to issue the command OpenStack token issue. If you get an error, it means that authentication failed.

A simple authentication verification is to issue the token issue command, as follows:

```
undercloud# source overcloudrc_danradez
undercloud# openstack token issue
```

Once you are able to authenticate, you can start to build your virtual infrastructure as a non-administrative user and create more accounts for other non-administrative users.

Interacting with Keystone in the dashboard

Now that we have worked through managing Keystone resources on the command line, let's take a look at how to do the same through the web interface. Connect to the dashboard and log in as the admin user using the password from the overcloudrc file. Select the **Admin** menu, and then select the identity submenu. Here, you'll see menu options to manage projects and users. Select the **Users** menu. You'll see the same list of users from the openstack user list command on the command-line. In the web interface, select the **Create User** button in the top-right corner of the **User Management** panel.

Fill in the form as appropriate:

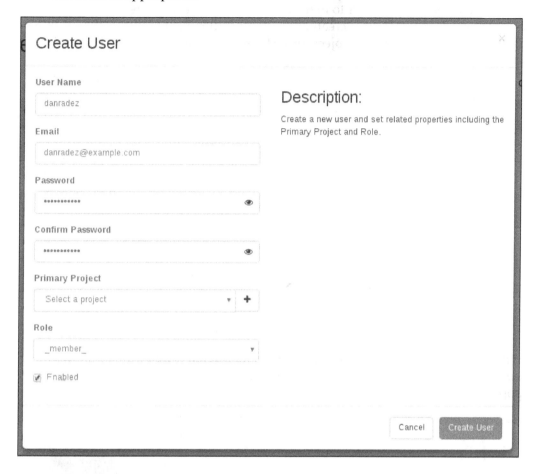

Before you can create the user, you'll have to select a project. If there isn't one that you want to add the new user to in the existing list, you can create one. Projects can be created inline of a user creation. Click the button next to the project selection drop-down menu. A **Create Project** form will show up as follows; fill this one in as appropriate:

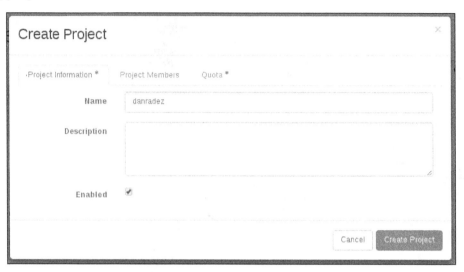

When you click on the **Create Project** button, the **Create User** form will show up again with all your original data filled in for you and the new tenant's name populated for you:

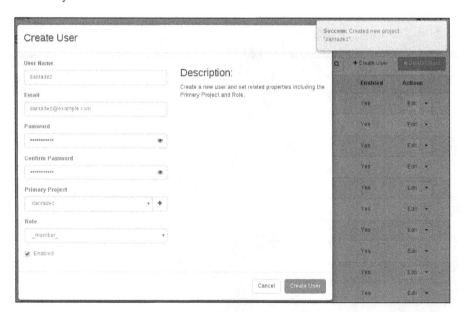

Now the user can be created. Click on **Create User**, and you're ready to start using the user's login and the new project. Remember that you can select an existing project instead of creating a new one. Using an existing one would just give your `nre` user access to the resources in an existing project.

Endpoints in the dashboard

We have looked at user management in the dashboard; now let's look at service and endpoints in the web interface. The dashboard does not provide a way to add or update services and endpoints. This is something reserved for the command line because it is usually done once and does not need any more management once it is done. Click on the **Project** menu and the **Access & Security** submenu. There will be a set of tabs to select from across the top of the screen, as shown in the following screenshot. Select **API Access**. Does this look familiar?

Access & Security

Security Groups   Key Pairs   Floating IPs   API Access

⬇Download OpenStack RC File v2.0   ➕View Credentials

Service	Service Endpoint
Compute	http://192.0.2.6:8774/v2/a2495cd5a42346a58cb3d14a772b6526
Network	http://192.0.2.6:9696/
Volumev2	http://192.0.2.6:8776/v2/a2495cd5a42346a58cb3d14a772b6526
Computev3	http://192.0.2.6:8774/v3
Image	http://192.0.2.6:9292/
Metering	http://192.0.2.6:8777/
Volume	http://192.0.2.6:8776/v1/a2495cd5a42346a58cb3d14a772b6526
Dashboard	http://192.0.2.6:80/dashboard/
Orchestration	http://192.0.2.6:8004/v1/a2495cd5a42346a58cb3d14a772b6526
Object Store	http://192.0.2.6:8080/v1/AUTH_a2495cd5a42346a58cb3d14a772b6526
Data Processing	http://192.0.2.6:8386/v1.1/a2495cd5a42346a58cb3d14a772b6526
Identity	http://192.0.2.6:5000/v2.0

Displaying 12 items

Summary

In this chapter, we looked at managing services, endpoints, users, projects, and roles through both the command line and the dashboard. Now that we have created users and assigned them roles in projects to manage virtual resources, let's start collecting the resources needed to launch an instance. The first resource that is needed before an instance can be launched is a disk image for that instance to launch from.

In the next chapter, we will look at Glance, the disk image management component, and how to import and build images to launch instances.

3
Image Management

In the preceding chapter, we looked at how identities are managed in OpenStack and how to authenticate to an OpenStack cluster. In this chapter, we will start to gather the resources necessary to launch an instance. The first resource we will work with is the image that an instance will use as its disk image when it is launched. Glance is the disk image management component in OpenStack. In this chapter, we'll look at how to register images with the image registry and how to build a custom cloud image.

Glance as a registry of images

At launch, a generic virtual machine requires a prebuilt disk image to boot from – some kind of storage that holds the operating system using which the virtual machine will run. Traditionally, a new virtual machine is created with a form of installation media accessible to it. This could take the form of an ISO, optical device, or maybe some form of network-accessible media. Whatever media is provided, an operating system installation is the next step in this scenario. One of the purposes of cloud computing is to be able to quickly create disposable virtual instances. The tasks of running an operating system installation and spawning a virtual machine fast are polar opposites of each other. Cloud computing has removed the need for a per-instance operating system installation by creating what have come to be known as cloud images. Cloud images are simply pre-installed bootable disk images that have been sealed. A sealed disk image is a sparse file containing a filesystem and an underlying operating system that has had its identifiable host-specific metadata removed. Host-specific items include things such as SSH host keys, MAC addresses, static IP addresses, persistent udev rules, and any other identifiers that would conflict if used by two of the same servers. Do you see where this is going? These images are imported into the Glance registry and then copied out to the compute nodes for the instances to launch with. We are going to first look at downloading a pre-baked image and registering it with Glance. Then, we'll look at what's needed to build your own custom image.

Downloading and registering an image

If you search the Internet for cloud image, you'll most likely get a link to a place to download a disk image from and import into Glance; most of the major distributions out there have one already built and ready to go for you. In general, they are distributed as **qcow2** or RAW images, and for the vast majority of cases, either of them will work fine. You will have to research them on your own to decide whether one or the other fits your use case better. There's also a test distribution, which is extra-super-small, called **CirrOS**. If you visit `http://download.cirros-cloud.net` download the `.img` file from the latest version is available.

 Don't use CirrOS for anything other than testing. It is built with libraries that make it insecure for anything other than demonstration and testing.

To demonstrate using Glance, we will use the Fedora qcow cloud image downloaded from `https://getfedora.org/`; let's start with the command line. To interact with Glance, you'll need to be sure that you have sourced your `overcloudrc` file; refer to *Chapter 2, Identity Management*, if you need a refresher on this. You will just get an authentication error message if an `overcloudrc` file is not currently sourced. Go ahead and list the images registered in Glance, as shown in the following command:

```
undercloud# openstack image list
```

This should return nothing since there aren't any images in Glance yet.

 It is important to note here that this command would only list the images in the project to which the user is authenticating.

When you have sourced your non-admin user's `overcloudrc` file, you would get the Glance images for that user's project. When you have sourced the admin user's `overcloudrc` file, you will see all tenants' Glance images. Next let's upload an image to Glance so that there's an image in Glance for us to list. To do this, use the `image-create` command. It is important to understand that you are not creating the disk image with this command. You need to have an already built image; use the `qcow2` file that you have just downloaded from Fedora. This `image create` command is creating a record of the image you are uploading in the Glance registry:

```
undercloud# openstack image create --public --disk-format qcow2
--container-format bare --file Fedora-x86_64-disk.qcow2 Fedora
```

You will notice that you can give your image a name other than the filename of the file that is being uploaded. The disk format and the container format are specific to the image file format that is being uploaded. There are other options for these parameters that you can use the OpenStack `help` command to read more about.

The public flag sets whether this image can be used across all tenants or is private to the tenant it is uploaded to. Now use the `image-list` command to list the image you just uploaded. Two images can have the same name; however, two images cannot have the same ID. There is also an argument that will protect the image from deletion and indicate that the image is protected (`--protected`). Administrators can't delete an image that is protected without first unprotecting the image. Let's use the `image set` command to set the image as protected. The following command captures the discussion in this paragraph:

```
undercloud# openstack image set --protected Fedora
```

In that example, the image's name was used to set the image as protected. It was mentioned that two images can have the same name; if they do, then the image's ID will have to be used instead of the image name. The properties for the images can be passed to `image create` or `image set`. Now that we've worked through using the command line to register a disk image with Glance, let's take a look at using the web interface.

Using the web interface

Next, let's use the web interface to add an image to the Glance image registry. Images can be managed by administrators and non-privileged users. On the command line, an image was added as the administrator. In the web interface, we will use the non-privileged user you have created. The following are the steps to add an image to the Glance image registry:

1. Log in to your web interface using the user you created in *Chapter 2, Identity Management*. Then, select **Images** from the menu. The following screenshot shows the **Images** page:

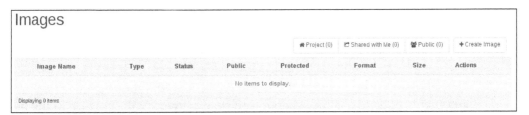

2. Once you are logged in, click on the **Create Image** button and fill out the form that appears (as shown in the following screenshot). All the options that were available on the command line are available in the web form:

3. Once the file has been uploaded, it will go through the status queued, saving and then will be registered when it is in state active, it will show up in the list of images, as shown in the following screenshot:

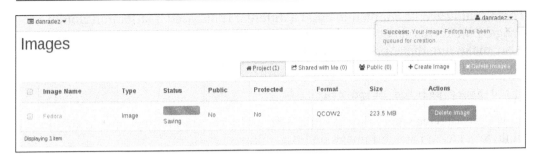

4. If you log back in as the admin user, you'll see all the imported images listed in the **Images** list under the admin menu. As the administrator, you can also pass the `--all-tenants` argument on the command line to see all the images that have been uploaded to the Glance registry.

Building an image

Now that we've looked at getting a disk image into Glance, let's investigate how a cloud image is built. A cloud image is just a sealed disk image with cloud-init included. A sealed disk image is a file that has an operating system installed in it and has had all the host-specific items removed from it. Cloud-init is a post-boot process that checks the metadata service of OpenStack and asks for post-boot commands that should be run on the launched instance. We'll see cloud-init's use cases in *Chapter 5, Instance Management*, and *Chapter 9, Orchestration*; for now, we'll just make sure it's included in the cloud image we build. To build the image, we'll use `virt-install`. There are quite a few other options. If you're familiar with a different disk-image-building tool, use that if you like. This is just one example of how to build one of these images. Go ahead and make sure `virt-install` is installed. The following command accomplishes this:

```
build-host# yum install -y virt-install httpd
```

`Httpd` was installed here too because we need a web server to serve the kickstart. Apache is not needed if you have an alternate web server to serve your kickstart. An automated Fedora installation is accomplished via the kickstart. A great place to get a baseline kickstart is from the collection of kickstarts at `https://git. fedorahosted.org/cgit/cloud-kickstarts.git/tree/generic/` that Fedora uses to build cloud images.

These could even be adapted to build a different rpm-based distribution cloud image. Pull down one of those kickstart files and place it in `/var/www/html/`. Also, make sure that Apache is running. Issue the following command to accomplish this:

```
build-host# service httpd start
```

Now that we have something to build with and a kickstart to define what should be built, let's kick off a cloud image build, as follows:

```
build-host# qemu-img create -f qcow2 my_cloudimage.img 10G
build-host# sudo virt-install -n my_cloud_image -r 2048 --vcpus=2 \
   --network=default --graphics=spice --noautoconsole \
   --noreboot -v --disk=path=my_cloudimage.img,format=qcow2 \
   -l http://dl.fedoraproject.org/pub/linux/releases/20/Fedora/x86_64/os/ \
   -x "ks=http://192.168.122.1/my_kickstart_file.ks"
```

The first command creates an empty `qcow2` formatted disk image. The second line spawns a virtual machine in `libvirt` named `my_cloud_image` with 2 GB of RAM and 2 vCPUs using the default `libvirt` network. The virtual machine boots using the kernel and the RAM disk in the install tree from the `dl.fedoraproject.org` URL. The `ks=` option is a kernel parameter. In this example, the kernel pulled from `dl.fedoraproject.org` knows how to pull down the kickstart being served from the local Apache instance on the `libvirt` network's gateway IP address. Once the installation is complete, the virtual machine can be torn down and the disk image that you created is now an installed cloud image. A final optional step is to sparsify the disk image. There is plenty of documentation on the Internet that can explain what it means to sparsify a disk image better than I can. Use your Internet-searching expertise to read more about what this command does and its benefits. To reiterate, this is optional and will not prevent the final image from being useful. Issue the following command to sparsify the disk image:

```
build-host# virt-sparsify --compress my_cloudimage.img
sparsified.qcow2
```

If you sparsified, the resulting sparsified disk image is what is imported into Glance. If you didn't sparsify, then just import the resulting disk image from `virt-installer`. Note that the `sparsify` command used the `.img` extension and the `.qcow2` extension. You can use these interchangeably. All the commands you run on these disk images don't really care what the file extension is as they inspect the contents of the disk image to complete their operations:

```
control# glance image-create --name Fedora --is-public true --disk-format
qcow2 -- container-format bare --file sparsified.qcow2
```

Now, let's be frank here. All that really happened was that an operating system was installed into a standard `qcow2` disk image with cloud-init included in the package list and the host's networking was set to DHCP. That means that if you want to do this manually instead of using `virt-install`, you could absolutely launch a virtual machine and do a manual installation. Then, make sure that cloud-init is installed and just before you shut down the machine, run commands to set the networking to DHCP and seal the image, somewhat like the following command:

```
cloud-image# cat > /etc/sysconfig/network-scripts/ifcfg-eth0 << EOF
DEVICE="eth0"
ONBOOT="yes"
BOOTPROTO="dhcp"
TYPE="Ethernet"
EOF
cloud-image# rm -f /etc/ssh/ssh_host*
cloud-image# rm /etc/udev/rules.d/70-persistent-net.rules
cloud-image# halt -p
```

The `udev` rule may not actually exist, but it doesn't hurt to make sure it's not there. What these commands do is remove any host-specific identification. The MAC address and ID are removed from the networking device configuration and the SSH host keys are removed. They're regenerated on boot if they don't exist, and the `udev` network persistence configuration is removed, which is also regenerated on boot if it's needed. This list is not exclusive. In the unlikely event that you come across other host-specific things, you should make sure that they are removed to make the image generic. However, on a fresh basic Fedora installation, this list should work well to seal the image. Once you've run these commands and shut down the virtual machine, the disk image is ready to be imported into Glance. If you boot the virtual machine back up outside of OpenStack, you will have to partially reseal the image, as some of the things you just deleted will be regenerated when you boot up using the disk image again. This does not apply to instances you boot in OpenStack. This only applies to manually spawning a virtual machine using the disk image outside of OpenStack. Once the image has been imported into Glance, OpenStack will handle things properly and not taint the Glance image. The imported image will be stored in the Glance registry and copied out to the compute nodes using which the instances will run. The instances will run using copies of the original disk images stored in Glance.

Summary

In this chapter, we looked at adding images to the Glance image registry for you to learn how to get a pre-baked Glance image and how to build your own Glance image. With a disk image stored in Glance, there is now a disk that the instances can copy and use to boot from the time they are spawned. Now that we have created users and stored disk images to launch with, the final resource that needs to be created before we launch an OpenStack instance is a virtual network. In the next chapter, we will use Neutron to create a virtual network fabric for an instance to be connected to.

4
Network Management

In the previous chapter, we prepared to launch an instance by importing disk images into Glance. The next preparation required for launching an instance is to create a virtual network for the instance to use. Neutron is the network management component in OpenStack. In this chapter, we'll look at how to create virtual networks and routers for the OpenStack instances to use. We will also look at some of the underlying plumbing that is used to support the virtual networks.

Networking and Neutron

As I was learning Neutron networking and started to present my experiences to audiences, I coined a phrase that I continue to stand by: *Networking is hard*. Networking is the most complex component in OpenStack and for good reason. This is because networking is a complex part of computing. It takes time and hard work to understand networking. It is often left to the network administrators and neglected by others. Hats off to you network administrators. I spent 7 years of my professional career avoiding learning some of the core concepts of networking and leaving it to the folks that did networking. OpenStack is where it caught up with me and bowled me over. To administer an OpenStack cloud that uses Neutron networking, you have to understand some of the core concepts used in networking. As we work through the rest of this book, I will make sure to explain these concepts as we come across them so that if you're not a networking guru, you will hopefully come out on the other side with an understanding that will equip you to administer your cloud well.

Using Neutron, you enable what is referred to as per-project or per-tenant networking. This means that virtual isolated networks can be created for each project, or more recently called projects. These networks only have routes to each other if you create them. These networks only have routes to the outside world if you create them, and there is next to nothing assumed about what an instance should be able to do on a network. This is important because it isolates the instances in different projects from each other. It is a security risk for an instance in network A to have access to an instance in network B by default, even if they are in the same project, though the default is for instances in the same network to have access to each other unless the network is specifically configured to behave differently. OpenStack was designed this way so that you would gain this security out of the box.

Network fabric

Neutron itself is an API that has a modular plugin architecture. The plugins interface with a networking fabric and manage that fabric for you. A networking fabric is just a fancy term for the physical underlying networking infrastructure and architecture that transports the data within a network. What this means is that Neutron by itself is kind of like a television remote by itself. Until the remote has a television that it can interface with and control, it is just a paperweight that your 2-year-old likes to spend time developing his fine motor skills with by pushing the buttons over and over. Similarly, until Neutron has a networking fabric tied to it that it can manage for you, it is basically useless.

There is a broad collection of vendors that have written plugins for Neutron to allow you to manage their compatible networking appliances. If you have a preferred networking vendor, ask them about their support for OpenStack Neutron. Investigating vendor support and configuration is beyond the scope of this book. Luckily, there is an open source virtual networking project that can meet the needs of our OpenStack networking installation.

Open vSwitch configuration

By default, the RDO installation you ran back in *Chapter 1*, *RDO Installation*, installed **Open vSwitch** (**OVS**), and configured the Neutron Open vSwitch plugin for you. Open vSwitch is virtual networking software that allows you to create virtual switches on your nodes and ties the virtual switches on your nodes together by way of a configured transport. A configured transport is a defined method for the virtual switches to talk to each other. As traffic comes out of an instance, it travels through these connections between each of the virtual switches. There are three common methods for configuring OVS, which are explained here.

VLAN

Virtual Local Area Network (VLAN) is the most complex to set up. This is because the hardware switch that carries your traffic must be configured properly to carry the VLAN tagging that is assigned to the traffic. When the network traffic is traveling through one of the virtual networks, it is assigned a VLAN tag, which is basically a numeric identifier. If the switch does not support this identifier to be attached to the traffic, it will not be carried from one virtual switch to another virtual switch, and the network separation is then lost. The benefit of this method is its efficiency. Because the VLAN tag is the only metadata being carried and is already a part of the packets being transferred, there is no additional overhead to using this method and it will provide you with the best performance.

GRE tunnels

Generic Routing Encapsulation (GRE) doesn't necessarily require special configuration in the physical switch connecting your nodes. This is because it encapsulates the traffic. Each node must have a direct established connection to every other node. This connection is a tunnel that hides the traffic being sent from the physical switch transporting it. This makes initial setup much easier, but it also comes with its own complexity. When networking traffic is transferred, it's divided into packets – just chunks of the network data being sent. This packet size by default is 1,500 bytes. This default size is known as the **Maximum Transmission Unit (MTU)**. The data being sent in a packet can be smaller than the MTU. The complexity comes in because to encapsulate or to identify a packet as a GRE packet, an extra header has to be added to each packet. If the data being transferred in the packet together with the GRE header is less than the MTU, then the packet passes through without any trouble. If the packet's data and the header are larger than the MTU, then fragmentation occurs. Fragmentation means that it takes two packets to transfer one packet's worth of data, and there is extra communication that has to happen to get the packets fragmented. In short, fragmentation is very bad for network load and throughput. Everything has an MTU. There are two ways to accommodate the GRE header, which are as follows:

- **Lower the instance's MTU**: If every instance boots with an MTU set on its network device that is low enough that when the GRE header is added, it doesn't exceed 1,500 bytes, then the rest of the network fabric can happily function at the default 1,500 MTU.

- **Enable jumbo frames**: This is the better, but more involved, option to configure. For the purpose of this book, we'll define jumbo frames as setting the MTU higher than the default 1,500 bytes. Using jumbo frames is preferable to modifying the instance's MTU because you have control over setting up jumbo frames. You will not have control over every instance that boots in your OpenStack cloud. You can try to use DHCP to send an MTU value for the instance to use, but not all operating systems will honor this value sent via DHCP. Jumbo frames have to be set up anywhere a GRE encapsulated packet will travel – mainly OVS and the physical switch connecting your OpenStack nodes.

VXLAN tunnels

VXLAN functions much like GRE. It's a tunnel that encapsulates the traffic by adding a header. The main difference is that it operates more like **User Datagram Protocol (UDP)** instead of like TCP. This eliminates some of the overhead of connections made between the nodes in your OpenStack cluster and is generally regarded as a more efficient tunneling approach than GRE. VXLAN requires the same accommodations for handling its headers that GRE does.

For simplicity's sake, we will lower the instance's MTU size to work around the header MTU size conflict in this book. We will do this by configuring DHCP to send a DHCP option to the instances telling them to use an MTU of 1,450. The header will fit comfortably in the 50 bytes of space we've created for it, and the packets will flow normally through the rest of the network that has GRE or VXLAN encapsulation. Be aware that this is not a 100 percent foolproof method. If the instance's operating system does not support accepting the DHCP option to lower the MTU, there is a chance that communication will not be established fully with the instance via its network device.

VXLAN with **OpenVSwitch (OVS)** is the default configuration in an RDO deployment. An alternative to OVS is to use the Linux Bridge agent, which only supports VXLAN overlay networks.

Creating a network

Now that we've explored some of the intricacies of what's happening under the hood, let's actually use Neutron to create a network by performing the following steps:

1. Log in to your control node and source your `overcloudrc` file; use the non-administrative user for this. The command to create a virtual network is as follows:

```
undercloud# openstack network create internal
undercloud# neutron subnet-create internal 192.168.37.0/24
```

That is it. You just created a virtual network. I know that for the length of the introduction we just covered, that was pretty anticlimactic. Note that when you create the subnet, you are adding it to the network named `internal` that you just created. It is important to note the difference in the two commands. The first uses the command structure that has been used thus far. The second one calls a command named after the component being configured, Neutron. OpenStack has been going through a slow transition from having a command-line client for each component to a converged CLI that standardizes the syntax for OpenStack command-line actions. You will see other places in this book that use the component's client instead of the converged client. This just means that the functionality being used has not been added to the converged CLI yet. Neutron is one of the components that have not been fully implemented and we will use the neutron-client instead of the openstack-client for the rest of the chapter.

The final argument to the `subnet-create` command is the **Classless Inter-Domain Routing (CIDR)** notation. If you are not familiar with it, you will have to search the Internet for an explanation of it. There are plenty of good ones. Also, search for the CIDR calculator; there are plenty of CIDR calculators on the Internet too.

 You can find a couple of examples of CIDR calculators at `http://jodies.de/ipcalc` and `http://www.subnet-calculator.com/cidr.php`.

In a CIDR calculator, you can type in the CIDR mentioned earlier and it will give you the usable IP range that it signifies. The CIDR that I've used, `192.168.37.0/24`, identifies a range of IP addresses from `192.168.37.1` to `192.168.37.254` with `192.168.37.255` as the broadcast address. This means that we can allocate IP addresses in this range for things on our network.

2. Next, let's list the network that we just created; you can also list the subnet. Here's how:

```
undercloud# openstack network list
undercloud# openstack subnet list
```

The subnet could have been created with a name. If it was, we could have updated it by referring to its name. Since one wasn't passed, the subnet's ID will have to be used, as follows:

```
undercloud# neutron subnet-create internal 192.168.37.0/24 --name
internal_subnet
```

3. Let's update the subnet by adding a **Domain Name System** (**DNS**) name server. The properties of a subnet and a network can be passed at the time of creation or updated later. Refer to the Neutron command-line help for more details. Here is how we update the subnet by adding a DNS name:

```
undercloud# neutron subnet-update {subnet-id-hash} --dns-
nameservers list=true 8.8.4.4 8.8.8.8
```

In *Chapter 3, Image Management*, we mentioned cloud-init. Cloud-init is the service that runs when an instance is booted and connects back to `169.254.169.254` to get metadata. SSH keys and post-boot scripts are two examples of what can be provided via metadata. This IP address is provided by Neutron and proxies the call from cloud-init to the metadata service.

4. Next, let's create a router and add the internal network as an interface to it:

```
undercloud# neutron router-create my_router
```

```
undercloud# neutron router-interface-add my_router {subnet-id-
hash}
```

Here again, had we passed the `--name` argument and given the subnet a name, we could have used that name instead of the subnet ID.

Web interface management

The web interface lets you create the network and subnet in the same dialog. Perform the following steps to obtain a network and a router:

1. Log in as your non-administrative user, select the **Network** menu, select the **Networks** submenu, and click on the **Create Network** button in the top-right corner, as shown here:

2. After you have filled in the network name, go to the next dialog screen and fill in the subnet information, as shown in the following screenshot:

3. In the final dialog box, add the DNS entries, as shown in the following screenshot:

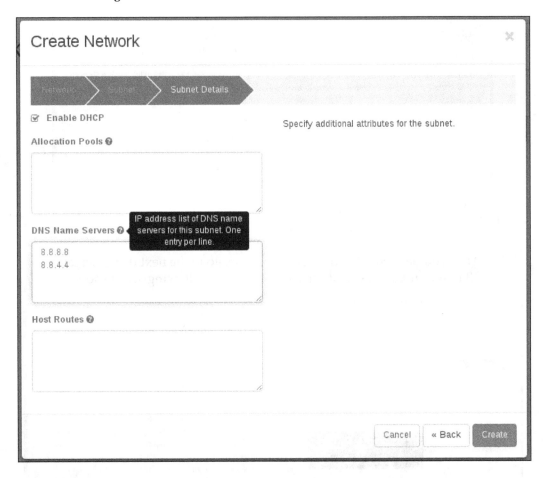

4. When you've completed filling in the dialog, you'll end up with a network and a subnet that's associated with the network, as shown in the following screenshot:

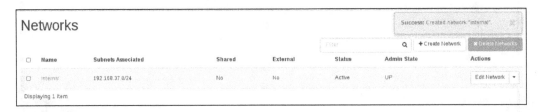

5. Next, create the router. Select **Routers** from the **Network** menu, and click on **Create Router** in the top-right corner of the page, as shown in the following screenshot:

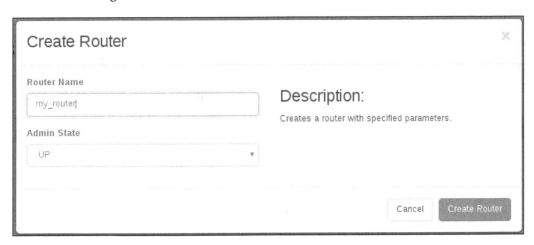

6. Once you've filled in the router name, click on **Create Router**, as shown in the following screenshot:

7. Next, click on the router's name, select the **Interfaces** tab and click on the **Add Interface** button in the top-right corner, as shown in the following screenshot:

8. Select the subnet on the network you created and add it as an interface to the router. Once the router has been created, there will be a success message in the upper-right corner, as shown in the following screenshot:

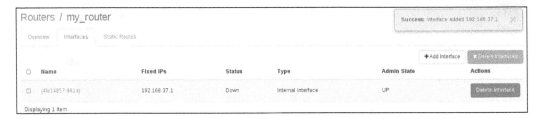

Now that we have a network and a router available, an instance can be launched and attached to the network. When the launched instance runs cloud-init, it will be able to connect to the metadata service to retrieve it's SSH keys. We'll launch the first instance when we get to *Chapter 5, Instance Management*. Before we do that, we have a little more networking to set up.

External network access

Every project will have at least one network to launch instances on, which will be built as we have just built a network. Whenever a new project is created, the steps that have just been performed will need to be performed for that new project. All projects will share a network that provides external access to the outside world. Let's work through creating this external network.

Preparing a network

Earlier, we discussed how Neutron is an API layer that manages virtual networking resources. The preparation for external network access will be different for different Neutron plugins. Talk to your networking vendor for your specific implementation. In general, what is being accomplished by this preparation is the connection of the networking node to a set of externally routable IP addresses. External just means external to, or outside of, the OpenStack cluster. These may be a pool within your company's 10.0.0.0/8 network or a pool of IPs public to the Internet. The project network IP addresses are not publicly routeable. The floating IP addresses allocated from the external network will be public and mapped to the project IP addresses on the instances to provide access to the instances outside of your OpenStack deployment. This is accomplished using the **Network Address Translation (NAT)** rules.

Since we are using Open vSwitch for this deployment, let's take a look at how OVS was set up by Triple-O when it was installed. Start by looking at the virtual switches defined on the control node. To do this, you will need to get the IP address of the control node. Get this from the undercloud. Source the stackrc file then ask Nova for a list of servers. We will do this again when we create instances in *Chapter 5, Instance Management*:

```
undercloud# source stackrc
undercloud# openstack server list
undercloud# ssh heat-admin@{ctlplane ip address}
overcloud-controller-0# sudo -i
overcloud-controller-0# ovs-vsctl show
5cd37026-4a3b-4601-b936-0143b0ef1545
    Bridge br-ex
        Port br-ex
            Interface br-ex
                type: internal
        Port phy-br-ex
            Interface phy-br-ex
                type: patch
                options: {peer=int-br-ex}
```

```
            Port "eth0"
                Interface "eth0"
        Bridge br-tun
            fail_mode: secure
            Port br-tun
                Interface br-tun
                    type: internal
            Port patch-int
                Interface patch-int
                    type: patch
                    options: {peer=patch-tun}
            Port "vxlan-c000020c"
                Interface "vxlan-c000020c"
                    type: vxlan
                    options: {df_default="true", in_key=flow, local_
ip="192.0.2.13", out_key=flow, remote_ip="192.0.2.12"}
        Bridge br-int
            fail_mode: secure
            Port int-br-ex
                Interface int-br-ex
                    type: patch
                    options: {peer=phy-br-ex}
            Port "tap39fb599f-25"
                tag: 1
                Interface "tap39fb599f-25"
                    type: internal
            Port br-int
                Interface br-int
                    type: internal
            Port patch-tun
                Interface patch-tun
                    type: patch
                    options: {peer=patch-int}
        ovs_version: "2.4.0"
```

In this output, you can see three bridges. You can think of each of these exactly as you would think of a switch – as a network appliance that has a bunch of places to plug in Ethernet cables into. A port is just something plugged into one of these virtual switch ports. Each of these virtual switches has a port to itself; br-int is patched to br-tun and br-tun is patched to br-int. You can see the VXLAN tunnel established between the control node and the compute node on br-tun. Br-int is known as the integration bridge and is used for local attachments to OVS. Br-tun is the tunnel bridge used to establish tunnels between nodes, and br-ex is the external bridge, which is what we need to focus on. Br-ex is important because it is patched to a physical interface on the control node. In the example previous, you can see eth0 as a port to br-ex. This is the device on your control node that can route traffic to the external pool of IP addresses. It is important when this happens to make sure that traffic flowing through the Ethernet device on the node communicates with OVS and not directly with the host itself. To make sure this happens, the IP address associated with the Ethernet device must be moved off the device and onto the OVS br-ex.

Next , look at the IP configuration for the host:

```
overcloud-controller-0# ip addr
1: lo: <LOOPBACK,UP,LOWER_UP> mtu 65536 qdisc noqueue state UNKNOWN
    link/loopback 00:00:00:00:00:00 brd 00:00:00:00:00:00
    inet 127.0.0.1/8 scope host lo
       valid_lft forever preferred_lft forever
    inet6 ::1/128 scope host
       valid_lft forever preferred_lft forever
2: eth0: <BROADCAST,MULTICAST,UP,LOWER_UP> mtu 1500 qdisc pfifo_fast
master ovs-system state UP qlen 1000
    link/ether 00:2c:8c:00:3a:af brd ff:ff:ff:ff:ff:ff
    inet6 fe80::22c:8cff:fe00:3aaf/64 scope link
       valid_lft forever preferred_lft forever
3: ovs-system: <BROADCAST,MULTICAST> mtu 1500 qdisc noop state DOWN
    link/ether 66:87:85:12:cf:b7 brd ff:ff:ff:ff:ff:ff
4: br-ex: <BROADCAST,MULTICAST,UP,LOWER_UP> mtu 1500 qdisc noqueue
state UNKNOWN
    link/ether 00:2c:8c:00:3a:af brd ff:ff:ff:ff:ff:ff
    inet 192.0.2.13/24 brd 192.0.2.255 scope global dynamic br-ex
       valid_lft 69570sec preferred_lft 69570sec
    inet 192.0.2.10/32 scope global br-ex
       valid_lft forever preferred_lft forever
    inet6 fe80::22c:8cff:fe00:3aaf/64 scope link
       valid_lft forever preferred_lft forever
5: br-int: <BROADCAST,MULTICAST> mtu 1500 qdisc noop state DOWN
    link/ether d6:c2:f6:fd:42:44 brd ff:ff:ff:ff:ff:ff
6: br-tun: <BROADCAST,MULTICAST> mtu 1500 qdisc noop state DOWN
    link/ether 2e:6e:05:fb:07:42 brd ff:ff:ff:ff:ff:ff
```

Notice here that the IP address you connected to with `ssh` is not on `eth0`; it is on `br-ex`. There are also virtual network devices for the other OVS bridges. There are also network configuration files in `/etc/sysconfig/network-scripts/`. Inspect the `ifcfg-eth0` and `ifcfg-br-ex` files and note the references to each other and to OVS.

[Triple-O does this networking setup for you. Packstack does not.]

Creating an external network

Now that you have explored the network plumbing that exposes OpenStack to the externally routable IP pool that will be managed by OpenStack, it is time to tell OpenStack about this set of resources it can manage. Because an external network is a general-purpose resource, it must be created by the administrator.

Exit your control node and source your `overcloudrc` file on your `undercloud` node so that you can create the external network as a privileged user. Then, create the external network, as shown in the following commands:

```
undercloud# neutron net-create --tenant-id service external
--router:external=True
undercloud# neutron subnet-create --tenant-id service external
192.0.2.0/24 --disable-dhcp --allocation_pool
start=192.0.2.100,end=192.0.2.199
```

You will notice a few things here. First, the project that the network and subnet are created in is the service project. As mentioned in *Chapter 2, Identity Management*, all resources are created in a project. General-purpose resources like these are no exception. They are put into the `service` project because users do not have access to networks in this project directly, so they would not have the ability to create instances and attach them directly to the external network. Things would not work if that was done because the underlying virtual networking infrastructure is not structured to allow this to work properly. Second, the network is marked as external. Third, note the allocation pools; the nodes are `101`, `102`, and `103`. So the IP addresses `100`–`109` are left out of the pool. This way, OpenStack will not allocate those IP addresses to the instances. Finally, DHCP is disabled. If DHCP was not disabled, OpenStack would try to start and attach a `dnsmasq` service for the external network. This should not happen because there may be a DHCP service running external to OpenStack that would conflict with the one that would have started if DHCP was enabled on the network you have just created.

The final step to make this network accessible to the instances in your OpenStack cloud is setting the project router's gateway to the external network. Let's do that for the router created earlier, as shown in the following command:

```
undercloud# neutron router-gateway-set my_router external
```

Web interface external network setup

Creating the external network can be completed through the web interface by performing the following steps:

1. Start by logging in to the web interface as the **Admin** user to create the external network and subnet. Select the **Networks** submenu from the **Admin** menu and click on **Create Network**. Give the network a name, flag it as external and make sure that it is assigned to the service project. The default provider type configured by Triple-O is VXLAN. On the command line, this was taken care of for you; here, select **VXLAN** for the **Provider Network Type** and set the **Segmentation ID** to 1. This step is encapsulated in the following screenshot:

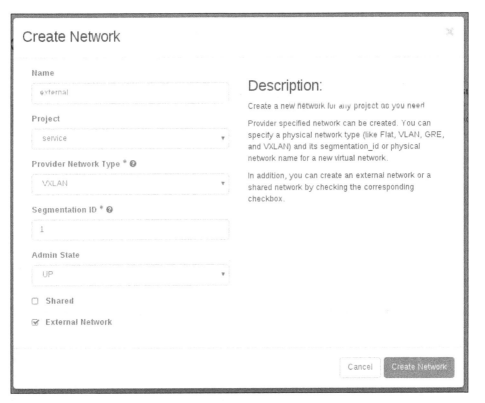

2. Once you have created the network, select the network by its name from the list, as shown in the following screenshot, and click on **Create Subnet**:

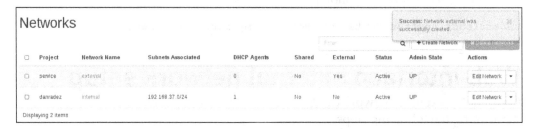

3. Fill out the form with the network information for the external pool of IP addresses. Make sure the correct gateway is specified. The following screenshot captures this step:

4. Move to the **Subnet Detail** dialog and make sure that you uncheck **Enable DHCP**. Fill in the allocation pool if necessary; if you are using the default Triple-O installation, set the allocation pool to `192.0.2.100,192.0.2.199`. This is only necessary when creating an external network as the administrative user and can be provided by your network administrator for a deployment being attached to a corporate network. This step is illustrated in the following screenshot:

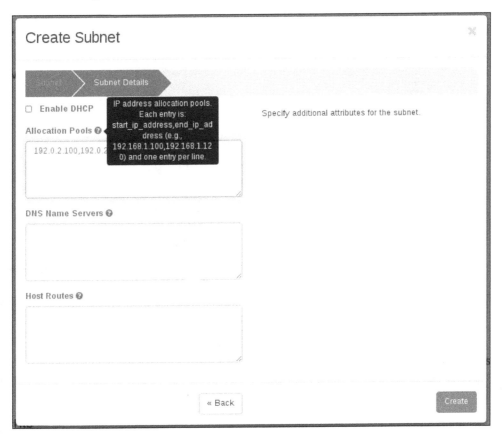

5. Once the subnet and network are created, as shown in the following screenshot, log out of the admin account and log back in as the non-privileged user:

6. Select the **Routers** menu options from the **Network** menu, click on the **Set Gateway** next to your router, and select the external network you just created as the admin user, as shown in the following screenshot:

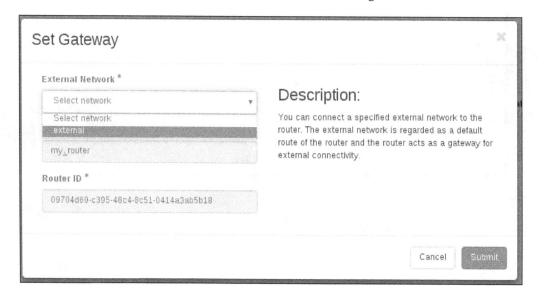

7. Once the router's gateway is set to the external network, everything will be in place to assign a floating IP address to an instance once it's launched, as shown in the following screenshot:

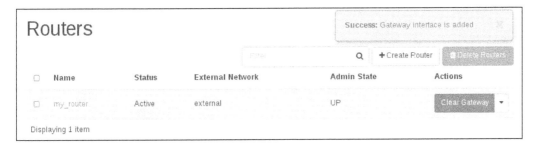

Summary

In this chapter, we looked at creating networks, subnets, and routers, and looked through the OpenVSwitch configuration used for this to work. Using these resources, the necessary virtual networking fabric has been created for an instance to be launched on. Now that we have created virtual networks for the instances to attach to, let's get into launching instances. In the next chapter, we will do what we have been working towards – launch an instance. We will use Nova to launch an instance from the image that was imported and attach it to these virtual networking resources.

5
Instance Management

In the past few chapters, we collected resources that laid the foundation to launch an instance. We have created a project – a place for our resources to live in. We added a disk image using Glance that the instance will use as its boot device. We created a network for the instance using Neutron. Now it is time to launch the instance. Nova is the instance management component in OpenStack. In this chapter, we will look at managing the following:

- Flavors
- Key pairs
- Instances
- Floating IPs
- Security groups

Managing flavors

When an instance is launched, there has to be a definition of the amount of resources that will be allocated to the instance. In OpenStack, this is defined by what are called **flavors**. A flavor defines the allocation of virtual CPUs, RAM, and disk space that an instance will use when it launches. When Triple-O installed your system earlier, it created a few flavors for you. Let's take a look at those. Go ahead and source an `overcloudrc` file. Once you have one sourced, list the flavors, as follows:

```
undercloud# openstack flavor list
```

You can create your own flavors if these do not fit your needs exactly, though only the admin user can create new flavors. There is nothing magical about the flavors that Triple-O has created. They have been created close to what the rest of the cloud industry uses for convenience. We are not going to get too deep into flavors; we'll just use the preconfigured flavors that you have just listed.

Managing key pairs

Since a cloud image is a copy of an already existing disk image with an operating system already installed, the root users are generally disabled, and if the root password is set, it is usually not distributed. To overcome the inability to authenticate without a password, OpenStack uses SSH key pairs. If you remember, in *Chapter 3*, *Image Management*, we discussed the need for cloud-init to be installed in a cloud image. Then, in *Chapter 4*, *Network Management*, we discussed how cloud-init would connect to the metadata service via the IP address provided by the router. One of the primary roles of this cloud-init process is to pull down the public SSH key that will be used for authentication. OpenStack provides a facility for you to manage your SSH key pairs so that you can select which will be used when you launch an instance. Let's start by generating a new key pair and listing it, as shown in the following commands:

```
undercloud# openstack keypair create my_keypair

-----BEGIN RSA PRIVATE KEY-----

{ truncated private key content }

-----END RSA PRIVATE KEY-----

undercloud# openstack keypair list
```

This has generated an SSH public/private key pair and listed the record of the key pair. The content that has been put on standard output should end up in a file in your home directory's SSH directory with a mode of 600. The private key just printed to standard out should be treated like a password. Do not share it, do not post it in public places. Keep it safe.

OpenStack has generated the key pair, given you the private key, and stored the public key to place on a future running instance. You could always redirect the output to a file so that you do not have to copy and paste. This is an alternative way to generate that key pair. The only difference is that the private key ends up in a file instead of being printed in the terminal. Issue the following command this way instead to accomplish this:

```
undercloud# openstack keypair create another_keypair > another.key
```

Once you have a file that contains the private key, for example, the other key file just created, you can drop this file into your ~/.ssh directory with a mode of 600. Then, that file is referenced to log in to a running instance that has the respective public key.

SSH key pairs are not anything specific to OpenStack. They are very commonly used in the Linux world. OpenStack supports the importing of an already existing public key. Let's walk through generating an SSH key pair outside of OpenStack and importing the public key into OpenStack, as shown in the following commands:

```
laptop$ ssh-keygen
Generating public/private rsa key pair.
Enter file in which to save the key (/home/dradez/.ssh/id_rsa):
/home/dradez/.ssh/openstack.rsa
Enter passphrase (empty for no passphrase):
Enter same passphrase again:
Your identification has been saved in
/home/dradez/.ssh/openstack.rsa.
Your public key has been saved in
/home/dradez/.ssh/openstack.rsa.pub.
The key fingerprint is:
4f:62:ee:b9:0f:97:35:f7:8a:91:37:84:0b:b9:cb:05 dradez@laptop
dradez@laptop:~$ ls -l /home/dradez/.ssh/openstack*
-rw-------. 1 dradez dradez 1675 /home/dradez/.ssh/openstack.rsa
-rw-r--r--. 1 dradez dradez  411
/home/dradez/.ssh/openstack.rsa.pub
```

As illustrated, on my laptop, I have generated a public/private key pair. You could do this on the undercloud if you wanted. The private key has a mode of 600, and the public key is the file that will be imported into OpenStack. In the OpenStack cluster, we are using the undercloud node to interact with the cluster. Copy the public key to your control node so that it can be imported, and import it into Nova, as shown in the following command:

```
undercloud# openstack keypair create --public-key openstack.rsa.pub
keypair_name
```

You can also manage key pairs in the web interface. In the **Compute** menu, select the **Access & Security** submenu. On this page, there will be a **Key Pairs** tab. You can click on **Create Key Pair** or **Import Key Pair** to manage key pairs through the web interface instead of on the command line. The following screenshot captures how we can manage key pairs in the web interface:

Launching an instance

At this point, there has been what may seem like an excessive amount of groundwork laid to get to launching an instance. We now have a project for the instance to live in, an image using which it can boot off, a network for it to live in, and a key pair to authenticate with. These are all the necessary resources to create in order to launch an instance, and now that these resources have been created, they can be reused for future instances that will be launched. Without further delay, let's launch the first instance in this OpenStack environment as follows:

```
undercloud# openstack server create --flavor 2 --image Fedora --key-name
openstack --nic net-id={internal net-id} "My First Instance"
```

This launches an instance using the small flavor, the key pair we just imported, the Fedora image from *Chapter 3, Image Management,* and the project network from *Chapter 4, Network Management.* This instance will go through a few different states before it is ready to use. You can see the current state of your instances by listing them as follows:

```
undercloud# openstack server list
```

This command will list the instances in your project. This list will include the ID of the instance, its name, its status and the networks that it is assigned to. Once the instance boot process completes, the instance will settle in an active state. The first time an instance boots, it will take an extra minute or two because the image file has to be copied from Glance to the hypervisor. Successive instance launches should happen in less than a minute.

Initially, the only communication you have with the instance is getting console logs or connecting to the console via Nova, as follows:

```
undercloud# openstack console log show "My First Instance"
undercloud# openstack console url show "My First Instance"
```

The first command will print the console log of the instance if it's available. This is useful to help debug why an instance won't start or to find out if it got an IP address from DHCP. The second command will give you a URL that can be loaded into your browser to give you a VNC console to the running instance.

Managing floating IP addresses

Now that an instance is running, the next step is to communicate with it in a fashion other than with the console through a web browser. In the instance list you just saw, an IP address on the tenant network will be listed once it's been assigned. The IP address that is initially assigned to the instance is not a routable IP address; to communicate with the instance, you will need to assign a floating IP address from the external network. The floating IP address will be mapped to the project network IP address, and you will be able to communicate with the instance by way of the floating IP address.

Before a floating IP address can be associated with an instance, it needs to be allocated to your project. Floating IP addresses are managed through Neutron, as follows:

```
undercloud# openstack ip floating create external
```

This allocates a floating IP address to the project. It uses the allocation pool from the external network that you created in *Chapter 4, Network Management*. Next, associate the floating IP address ID with the port ID, as follows:

```
control# openstack ip floating add {ip_address} "My First Instance"
```

When the association is complete, a fixed IP will be listed next to the floating IP when you show a list of allocated floating IPs. The floating IP will also be listed in the networks field next to the project network IP address for your instance:

```
controlundercloud# openstack ip floating list
undercloud# openstack server list
```

Managing security groups

At this point, you may think that you should be able to connect to your instance. Not quite yet. There is a layer of security built into OpenStack called **security groups**. Security groups are firewalls that can be assigned to one or more instances. You can define multiple security groups; you can assign multiple instances to a security group; you can even assign multiple security groups to a running instance. A security group named default is created for each project when the tenant is created. List the existing security groups and you will see multiple with a description *Default security group*. Then list the rules in the project you are authenticating to:

```
undercloud# neutron security group list
undercloud# openstack security group rule list
```

If you list all projects that exist and get their IDs, they should map to the project IDs that the security groups you have just listed are assigned to. When you list the rules defined in a security group and do not pass a specific project, you will get a list of the rules in the project you are authenticating to. If you want to see the rules for a specific security group, just pass the UUID of the security group you are interested in; grep is a good tool for this once your project list grows larger. Here are the commands to grep the ID of the project created in *Chapter 2*, *Identity Managment,* then get the security group ID of the project's default security group and finally to list its security group rules:

```
undercloud# openstack project list | grep danradez

undercloud# openstack security group list | grep {uuid_of_project}

undercloud# openstack security group rule list {uuid_of_sec_group}
```

As you can see, the default rules added to the default security group are pretty basic and the output from this list is very empty. The rules there restrict all incoming traffic from the outside. Ingress is incoming traffic to an instance; and only incoming traffic from within the security group itself is allowed. Egress is outgoing traffic; all outgoing traffic is allowed by default. Let's add a few rules to allow some external traffic to connect to the instance:

```
undercloud# openstack security group rule create --proto tcp --dst-port
22 default
```

This rule will allow all incoming SSH traffic on port 22 to be passed to instances in the default security group. If you try this with the admin's overcloudrc file sourced, you will add the rule to the admin project. If with the project you created, then it will be added to that project's default security group. Let's add a rule to allow us to ping the host too:

```
undercloud# openstack security group rule create --proto icmp default
```

As mentioned earlier, you can also have more than one security group. You can create a new security group with Neutron's `security-group-create` command, as follows:

`undercloud# openstack security group create new_secgroup`

If, for some reason, the default group did not get created, that command could add it for you if you name it default. If you create additional security groups, then other rules could be added to those groups, for example, a rule to allow access to port 80 for web traffic:

`undercloud# openstack security group rule create --proto tcp --dst-port 80 new_secgroup`

Now, when an instance is launched, the option `--security-groups` could be passed. The value given to it could be `default` or `new_secgroup` or `default,new_secgroup`. The respective traffic would be allowed based on what combination of security groups was assigned to the new instance being booted. If you do not pass this option, the default security group will automatically be the group assigned to the new instance.

Communicating with the instance

The instance we booted was assigned the default security group. Edits made to a security group are immediately applied to the instances operating in them. We just added the ping and SSH rules to allow incoming traffic to the instances running in the default security group, so you should be able to ping and SSH to the instance you launched. Here is the output summary:

```
undercloud# ping -c 3 192.0.2.101
PING 192.0.2.101 56(84) bytes of data.
64 bytes from 192.0.2.101: icmp_seq=1 ttl=64 time=0.040 ms
64 bytes from 192.0.2.101: icmp_seq=2 ttl=64 time=0.041 ms
64 bytes from 192.0.2.101: icmp_seq=3 ttl=64 time=0.040 ms
--- 192.0.2.101 ping statistics ---
3 packets transmitted, 3 received, 0% packet loss, time 1999ms
rtt min/avg/max/mdev = 0.040/0.040/0.041/0.005 ms
undercloud# ssh fedora@192.0.2.101
The authenticity of host '' 192.0.2.101 (192.0.2.101)'' can''t be
established.
RSA key fingerprint is 83:d8:f4:7e:01:db:4e:50:8a:bd:f6:dc:77:2c:31:d7.
Are you sure you want to continue connecting (yes/no)? yes
Warning: Permanently added ''192.0.2.101'' (RSA) to the list of
known hosts.
[fedora@my-first-instance ~]$
```

Launching an instance using the web interface

Now that we've booted an instance on the command line, let's take a look at doing the same thing in the web interface:

1. Go ahead and log in to the web interface as the non-administrative user you created in *Chapter 2, Identity Management*.

2. Under the **Compute** menu, select **Instances** and then click on the **Launch Instance** button.

3. In the **Launch Instance** dialog, start by filling in a name for the instance, as shown in the following screenshot. Also, note that there are blue asterisks next to **Source**, **Flavor**, and **Networks**. These are the required sections of the dialog to visit:

4. Click the **Next** button to get to the **Source** section of the dialog. There will be a **+** button next to the Fedora image you uploaded in *Chapter 3, Image Management*. Click that to select the Fedora image as the boot source for the instance, as shown in the following screenshot:

5. Click the **Next** button to get to the **Flavor** section of the dialog. There will be a **+** button next to the available flavors. Select the **m1.small** flavor, as shown in the following screenshot:

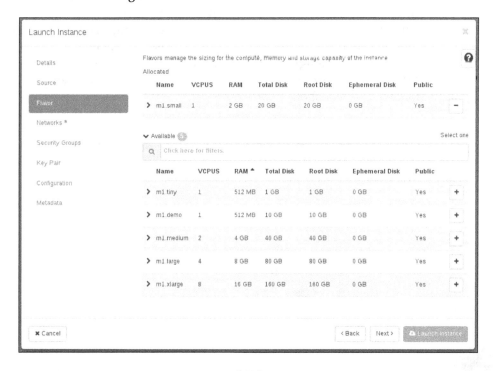

6. Click the **Next** button to get to the **Networks** section of the dialog. There will be a **+** button next to the **internal** network you created in *Chapter 4, Network Management*. Select the **internal** network, as shown in the following screenshot:

7. Click the **Next** button to get to the **Security Groups** section of the dialog. There will be a **+** button next to the **default** security group. This section was not highlighted with a blue asterisk. This is because the default security will be automatically assigned to your instance if it is the only one that exists. Select the **default** security group if you would like to, as shown in the following screenshot:

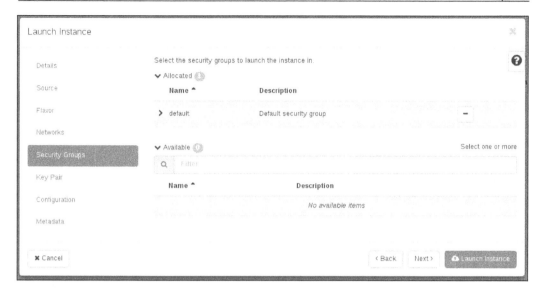

8. Click the **Next** button to get to the **Key Pairs** section of the dialog. There will be a **+** button next to the key pair you created or imported. This section was not highlighted with a blue asterisk. This is because a key pair is not a strict requirement to launch an instance. If one is not selected, one will not be installed on the instance and other means of authentication will need to be used to connect to the instance. Select your key pair if you would like to, as shown in the following screenshot:

9. Finally, click the **Launch Instance** button for the instance to be launched, as shown in the following screenshot:

10. Click on the instance's name; there is a **Log** tab and a **Console** tab. The **Log** tab will load the system message log from the instance. This is the same content that was displayed by the `openstack console log show` command executed in the *Launching an Instance* section earlier. Here's a screenshot of this page:

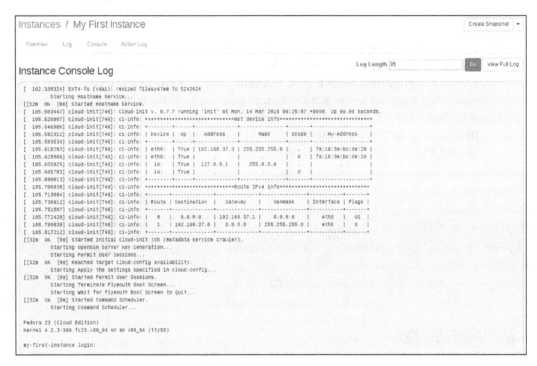

11. The **Console** tab will provide an in-browser vnc session to the instance. You must be able to connect to port 6080 to see this console. OpenStack exposes a service on 6080 that handles proxying the VNC sessions into the instances. The next step is to associate a floating IP address to the instance. To the right of the instance, there is a drop-down menu that has the option **Associate Floating IP**. If the instance is still spawning and has not quite become active, this menu option may not be available right away. Once you can select this option, a dialogue will display, as shown in this screenshot:

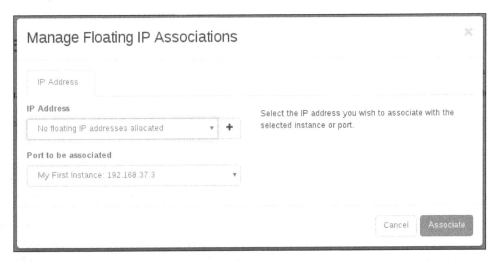

12. Remember that a floating IP first needs to be allocated to a project before it can be associated with an instance. Click on the **+** button next to the IP address selection box. This will display a dialog to allocate a floating IP, as shown in the following screenshot:

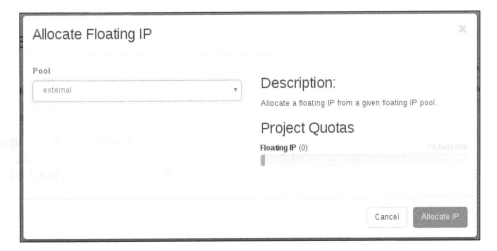

13. Click on **Allocate IP** to allocate an IP to your project. The original dialog to associate the floating IP will display again with the newly allocated floating IP address populated in the **IP Address** box, as shown in the following screenshot:

14. Click the **Associate** button to complete the association. The web browser may take you to the **Access & Security** screen, where floating IPs are managed. The associate will be indicated next to the floating IP address. Return to the **Instances** list; once the floating IP has been associated, it will show up in the **IP Address** box next to the instance. This is not an auto-update piece of information. If you do not see it there right way, refresh your browser after a few seconds to see the update. The following screenshot captures this step:

15. The final step is to open up ports to the instance through the security groups. Click on the **Access & Security** menu, select the **Security Groups** tab, and click on the **Manage Rules** button. In the top-right corner, click on the **Add Rule** button.

16. Fill out the form for ICMP, as shown in the following screenshot:

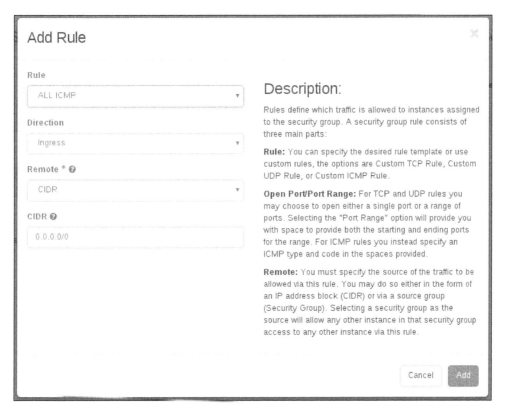

17. Repeat this for SSH and for any other port you need opened up.

Summary

In this chapter, we looked at managing flavors, key pairs, instances, security groups, and floating IP addresses. Now that we have a running OpenStack instance, let's attach some virtual storage to it. A running instance's storage is ephemeral by design. This means that any data stored in the instance's local disk is lost upon the instance's termination. In the next chapter, we will attach a virtual block storage device to the running instance. This storage will persist after an instance that it is attached to is terminated.

6
Block Storage

Cinder is the block storage component in OpenStack. In the previous chapter, all the necessary resources were collected to launch an instance. Now that this instance is running, let's look at the use case for block storage and the process of attaching virtual block storage to the OpenStack instance. Then, we will take a look at the storage engine used to store these block devices and the other options available for the backing store.

Use case

OpenStack instances run on ephemeral disks – disks that only exist for the life of the instance. When an instance is terminated, the disk is discarded. This is a problem if there is any information that requires persistence. Block storage is one type of storage that can be used to persist data beyond the termination of an OpenStack instance.

Using Cinder, users can create block devices on demand and present them to running instances. The instances see this as a normal, everyday block device – as if an extra hard drive was plugged into the machine. The extra drive can be used as any other block device by creating partitions and filesystems on it. Let's look now at how to create and present a block storage device using Cinder.

Creating and using block storage

Creating a block device is as simple as specifying the size and a name for the block device being created:

```
undercloud# openstack volume create --size 1 my_volume
```

This command created a virtual block device that is 1 GB of storage space. To see the devices, use the `list` command:

```
undercloud# openstack volume list
```

The volume will be listed with information about it. As with the components already covered, the admin user can see all volumes that are in Cinder and non-privileged users see only the Cinder volumes in their project. When volumes are created, they cycle through a progression of states that indicate the status of the new block device. When the status reaches *Available*, it is ready to be attached to an instance.

Attaching the block storage to an instance

The virtual storage device we just created is not much good to us unless it is attached to an instance that can make use of it. Luckily for us, we just launched an OpenStack instance and logged in to it. Perform the following steps to attach the block storage to an instance:

1. To show the attachment, start by connecting to the instance and listing the existing block devices on the instance that is running:

   ```
   instance# ls /dev/vd*

   /dev/vda   /dev/vda1
   ```

   The boot device for this instance is vda; this is the Glance image that was used to boot.

2. Now attach the volume you just created to the instance you have running. When you list the devices on the instance again, you will see the Cinder volume show up as vdb:

   ```
   undercloud# openstack server add volume "My First Instance" my_
   volume

   instance# ls /dev/vd*

   /dev/vda   /dev/vda1   /dev/vdb
   ```

3. The Cinder volume was attached as vdb to the instance. Now that we have a new block device on the instance, we treat it just as we would any other block device. Make a partition, create a file system, mount it, and read and write to it. The output from the following commands will be truncated for brevity:

   ```
   instance# fdisk /dev/vdb

   Command (m for help): n

   Partition type:
       p    primary (0 primary, 0 extended, 4 free)
       e    extended
   Select (default p): p
   ```

```
Partition number (1-4, default 1): 1

First sector (2048-2097151, default 2048):

Last sector, +sectors or +size{K,M,G,T,P} (2048-2097151,
default 2097151):

Created a new partition 1 of type 'Linux' and of size 1023
MiB.

Command (m for help): w

The partition table has been altered.

instance# mkfs -t ext4 /dev/vdb1

Writing superblocks and filesystem accounting information:
done

instance# mount /dev/vdb1 /mnt

instance# echo "test" > /mnt/test

instance# cat /mnt/test

test
```

4. Let's unmount the device and detach it from the running instance:

```
instance# umount /mnt

undercloud# openstack server remove volume "My First Instance" my_
volume

instance# ls /dev/vd*

/dev/vda   /dev/vda1
```

In these steps, we showed that only vda exists on the instance. Next, we attached the volume and showed you how the instance sees it as vdb. Then, we partitioned, mounted, and wrote to the file system. Finally, the device was unmounted and detached, and it was shown that vdb has been removed. If the volume was reattached, there would be no need to partition it and create a file system. Data written to the volume will persist as long as the volume exists.

Managing Cinder volumes in the web interface

Now that we have used the command line to manage Cinder volumes, let's take a look at using the web interface to accomplish the same thing:

1. Log in to the web interface as your non-administrative user and select the **Volumes** submenu from the **Compute** menu.

2. In the top-right corner, click on the **Create Volume** button.

3. Fill in the name and size and click on **Create Volume** on the form:

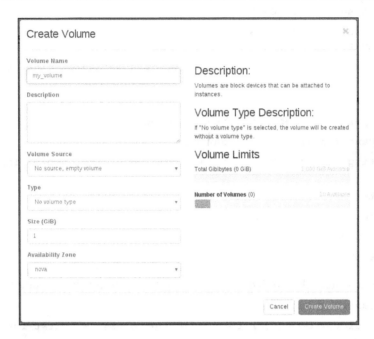

4. The web interface will update itself as the volume status changes. Once it becomes available, click on the **More** menu on the volume page and select **Edit Attachments**. In this dialog, the volume will be connected to the running instance. The following screenshot captures this step:

5. In the **Attachments** dialog, select the instance to attach the volume to and click on the **Attach Volume** button, as shown in the following screenshot:

6. Once again, the web interface will get updated as the status of the volume changes. The volume's status will become **In-Use** when it is attached to the instance and ready for the initial partitioning and file system creation. The following screenshot encapsulates this step:

7. To detach the volume, open the **Edit Attachments** dialog in the **More** menu and click on **Detach Volume**. The status of the volume will return to *Available* once the detach process is complete. The following screenshot captures this step aptly:

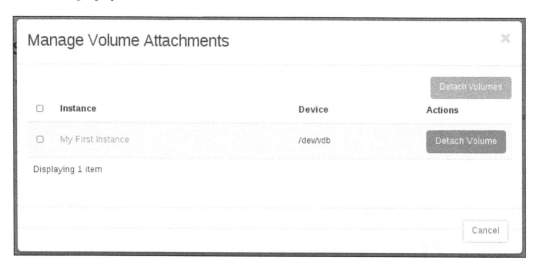

Backing storage

Now that you have seen how to use Cinder, you may be wondering where that volume that was created was stored. The cloud may be a facade of endless resources, but the reality is that there are actual physical resources that have to back the virtual resources of the cloud. By default, Cinder is configured to use LVM as its backing store. In *Chapter 1, RDO Installation*, Ceph was indicated for configuration. If that had not been done, Triple-O would have created a virtual disk and mounted it as a loopback device on the control node to use as the LVM physical volume to create a cinder-volumes volume group. The Cinder volume you just created would have been a logical volume in the cinder-volumes volume group. This is not an ideal place to store a virtual storage resource for anything more than a demonstration. Using a virtual disk mounted as a loopback device has very poor performance and will quickly become a bottleneck under load.

Cinder types

There are many different types of storage that can be used to back Cinder. LVM is an easy choice, although software-defined solutions, such as Ceph and GlusterFS, are also very popular. Another option would be to engage your favorite hardware storage vendor as you ask them about their support for Cinder storage. When multiple backing storage solutions are used in Cinder, they are defined and referred to as types. To demonstrate this, let's add GlusterFS as another backing store option type to our OpenStack cluster.

Ceph setup

Triple-O has built-in support to deploy a Ceph cluster and use it as the primary backing store for Cinder and for Glance. In *Chapter 1, RDO Installation*, there was a ceph parameter and a storage environment file that were passed to the overcloud deployment command. They set up Ceph as the backing store for your Triple-O deployment. If you left those two options out of the deployment command, Triple-O would default back to LVM as the backing store for Cinder.

GlusterFS setup

This demonstration shows an example starting with an LVM-configured backing store. If you would like to do this example, you will need to start with a deployment that has LVM configured and not Ceph.

Conveniently enough, a simple GlusterFS installation is not extremely complicated to set up. Assume three rpm-based Linux nodes named gluster1, gluster2, and gluster3 with an sdb drive attached for use by a GlusterFS storage cluster. The file system XFS is recommended although an ext4 file system will work fine in some cases. Research the pros and cons of each file system related to GlusterFS before you deploy a production GlusterFS storage cluster. Create a partition and a file system on the sdb disk. We'll begin our demonstration for this book by mounting the disk, and creating and starting the GlusterFS volumes. The following steps should be performed on each of the GlusterFS nodes:

1. Start by preparing the host and installing GlusterFS:

   ```
   # mkdir -p /export/sdb1 && mount /dev/sdb1 /export/sdb1

   # echo "/dev/vdb1 /export/vdb1 ext4 defaults 0 0" >>
   /etc/fstab

   # yum install -y glusterfs{,-server,-fuse,-geo-replication}
   ```

2. The following commands should be run only on one node as they propagate across the GlusterFS storage cluster via the Gluster services:

    ```
    # service glusterd start
    # gluster peer probe gluster2
    # gluster peer probe gluster3
    # gluster volume create openstack-cinder rep 3 transport tcp
    gluster1:/export/vdb1 gluster2:/export/vdb1
    gluster3:/export/vdb1
    # gluster volume start openstack-cinder
    # gluster volume status
    ```

    The last command should show you the Gluster volume you just created and the bricks that are being used to store the GlusterFS volume openstack-cinder. What these commands set up is a three-node Gluster installation where each node is a replica. That means that all the data lives on all three nodes. Now that we have GlusterFS storage available, let's configure Cinder to know about it and present it to the end user as a backing storage option for Cinder volumes.

3. Now that GlusterFS is set up, we need to tell Cinder about setting up the Cinder volume types. Let's configure Cinder to use GlusterFS as a backing store. Start by editing /etc/cinder/cinder.conf; make sure that the enable_backends option is defined with the following values and that the respective configuration sections are defined in the file:

    ```
    enabled_backends=my_lvm,my_glusterfs

    [my_lvm]
    volume_group = cinder-volumes
    volume_driver = cinder.volume.drivers.lvm.LVMISCSIDriver
    volume_backend_name = LVM
    [my_glusterfs]
    volume_driver = cinder.volume.drivers.glusterfs.GlusterfsDriver
    glusterfs_shares_config = /etc/cinder/shares.conf
    glusterfs_sparsed_volumes = false
    volume_backend_name = GLUSTER
    ```

The `my_lvm` definition preserves the existing LVM setup that has already been used to create a Cinder volume. The `my_glusterfs` section defines options to attach to the GlusterFS storage we have just configured. You will also need to edit the `/etc/cinder/shares.conf` file. This file defines the connection information to the GlusterFS nodes. Reference the first and second Gluster nodes in the `shares.conf` file. It contains the following line:

```
gluster1:/openstack-cinder -o backupvolfile-
server=gluster2:/openstack-cinder.
```

4. Next, you'll need to restart the Cinder services to read the new configurations added to the `cinder.conf` file:

```
control# service openstack-cinder-scheduler restart
control# service openstack-cinder-volume restart
control# mount | grep cinder
gluster1:openstack-cinder on /var/lib/cinder/... type
fuse.glusterfs
gluster2:openstack on /var/lib/cinder/... type fuse.glusterfs
```

5. The `mount` command shown here just verifies that Cinder has automatically mounted the Cinder volumes defined. If you don't see the Cinder volumes mounted, then something has gone wrong. In that case, check the Cinder logs and the Gluster logs for errors to troubleshoot why Cinder couldn't mount the Gluster volume. At this point, the backing stores have been defined, but there is no end user configuration that has been exposed. To present the end user with this new configuration, Cinder type definitions must be created through the API:

```
control# cinder type-create lvm
control# cinder type-key lvm set volume_backend_name=LVM
control# cinder type-create glusterfs
control# cinder type-key glusterfs set
volume_backend_name=GLUSTER
control# cinder type-list
```

6. Now there are two types available that can be specified when a new volume is created. Further, when you list volumes that are in Cinder, they will have a volume type corresponding to which backing store is being used for each volume:

```
control# cinder-create --volume-type glusterfs 1
control# cinder list
```

7. The next time you create a new volume in the web interface, the two types will be available for selection on the volume creation dialog.

Summary

In this chapter, we looked at creating Cinder volumes and adding an additional storage type definition. Cinder block storage is just one virtual storage option available. In the next chapter, we will take a look at the Swift object storage system to compare the storage options available to OpenStack instances. Cinder offers block storage that attaches directly to the instances. Swift offers an API-based object storage system. Each storage offering has its advantages and disadvantages and is chosen to meet specific needs in different use cases. It is important to know how each of these works so that you can make an informed decision about which is right for you when the time comes to choose a storage solution.

7
Object Storage

In the previous chapter, we looked at managing block storage with Cinder. Block storage attaches directly to the instances, and the operating system on the instance writes to the filesystem. Object storage is an alternative storage option. Object storage is a simple form of storage that handles file operations on the instances by way of API calls. This decouples the operating system and the file storage. Swift is the object storage component in OpenStack. In this chapter, we are going to take a deeper look at what object storage is, how to use it, and some options available to use as the backend storage engine.

Use case

Object storage works by using a client to send and receive files to and from the object store. The files are stored with very little metadata and are treated as a whole entity. The object server does not work in partial pieces of an object the way block storage would work with file blocks. It is a very simple storage method focused on storing and retrieving the contents of the files with minimal overhead to the operating system while interacting with the storage server. The power of the Swift object storage engine is its robust software-defined storage backend. The Swift storage engine has distribution and replication capabilities across its storage nodes. First, let's take a look at the client side of using Swift, and later, we will look at the backend storage engine.

Architecture of a Swift cluster

Swift has a proxy layer and a storage layer. These layers are associated with each other by way of the ring. The ring is a catalog of the objects that are being stored in the cluster and where they are being stored. This information is replicated to every storage node to improve the performance of the cluster. The proxy layer is a service that presents an API interface to end users and communicates with the storage layer on behalf of the end user. The storage layer is not generally communicated with directly.

By default, Swift uses the Swift storage engine for its storage backend. The Swift storage is a storage engine designed specifically for the Swift object storage cluster that is distributed in nature and able to be replicated. The Swift storage engine has a few subcomponents to it: the account server, the object server, and the container server.

Swift can also be backed by storage engines other than the Swift storage engine. There are a few other storage solutions that have integration with Swift. Ceph and GlusterFS are two examples.

Each object stored in Swift is associated with a container, and containers are owned by an account. These associations are stored in the ring; there is a separate ring file for each of the accounts, containers, and objects.

Creating and using object storage

The two main concepts when using Swift are containers and objects. Containers are groups of files that contain objects. Objects are simply files and must exist inside of a container. Make sure that your overcloudrc file is sourced, then create a container and upload a file to the container. Let's use the release file from the etc directory as an example file to upload:

```
undercloud# openstack container create my_container
undercloud# openstack object create my_container /etc/redhat-release
undercloud# openstack container list
undercloud# openstack object list my_container
```

Once the container and the object are created, they can be listed with the respective list command. Next, upload the same file, but change to the etc directory first and reference it by just its filename, as follows:

```
undercloud# cd /etc
undercloud# openstack object create my_container redhat-release
undercloud# openstack object list my_container
```

Note the difference in how the object gets named according to how you reference the file in the `object create` command. It is important here to understand that there is not a directory structure in object storage. The filename just has a slash in it. Be aware that if you address a file in a subfolder when you upload it, the path to the file being uploaded will be included in the name of the object that is created to store the uploaded object. There is no reason not to use a directory structure style denotation in your file naming conventions. The point here is that it is just a naming convention and not a directory structure as it would be with an actual filesystem.

Object file management in the web interface

Now, let's take a look at managing containers and objects in the web interface. Once you have logged in, open the **Object Store** menu and select the **Containers** submenu. Click on the **Create Container** button. The following screenshot captures this step:

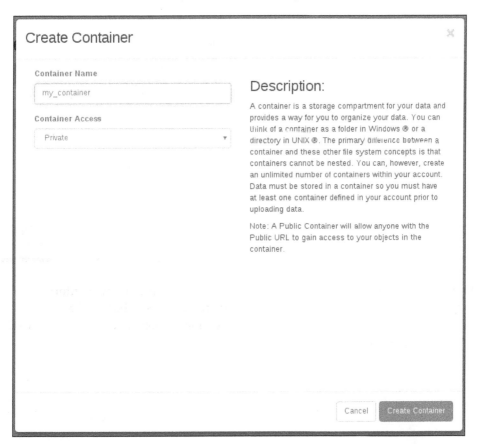

Now you will be presented with the following screenshot:

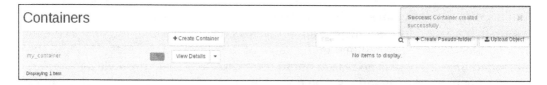

Once you have a container created, you will have two buttons to choose from to create objects in the container, **Create Pseudo Folder** and **Upload Object**. Start with uploading an object, as shown in the following screenshot:

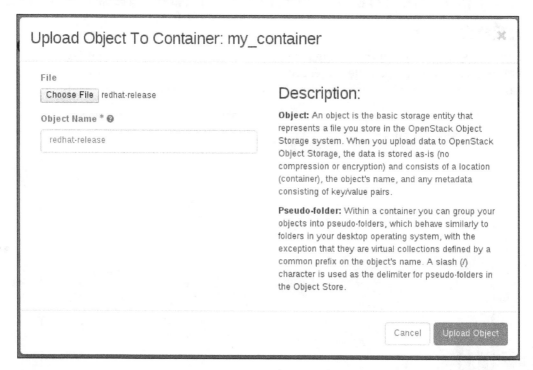

The file that was chosen was /etc/redhat-release again. The web interface prepopulates the object name field with the file name chosen but not its path. Click **Upload Object** to complete the object creation. These actions are illustrated in the following screenshot:

A directory-structure-like name could have been given to the object when it was uploaded. To offer assistance with using a convention that would mock a file system's directory structure, the **Create Pseudo-folder** button is provided. Click the **Create Pseudo-folder** button and create a test pseudo-folder. The following screenshot shows us the result:

Once a pseudo-folder is created, it can be clicked and drilled down into. Any object uploaded would then be named with a prefix of the selected pseudo-folder's name.

Using object storage on an instance

Now that we have seen how to get files in and out of Swift, let's look at installing the necessary client libraries on an instance to be able to interact with object storage on the instance. We will need to have the Swift client libraries installed so that the OpenStack command-line client can be executed on an instance. In this cluster, Swift is using Keystone for authentication. Swift can also use other authentication. It has a built-in authentication system and can also be used with other common authentication systems. Since Swift is configured to use Keystone for authentication, the Keystone client will also need to be installed. Let's install those clients now:

```
instance# sudo yum install -y https://www.rdoproject.org/repos/rdo-
release.rpm
instance# sudo dnf install -y python-openstackclient
```

There will be a quite a few dependent packages that yum will install. Once those are installed, you will need to create a `keystonerc` file to source. Create a file with the same information that was used to create the `overcloudrc` file. The names of these `rc` files do not matter. The filename `keystonerc` is a traditional name for these files that hold this authentication information:

```
instance# cat > ~/keystonerc_danradez << EOF
export OS_USERNAME=danradez
export OS_TENANT_NAME=danradez
export OS_PASSWORD=supersecret
export OS_AUTH_URL=http://192.168.122.101:5000/v2.0/
export PS1='[\u@\h \W(keystone_danradez)]\$ '
EOF
```

Make sure that the `auth_url` matches the `auth_url` from your original `overcloudrc` file. Once you have this file, source it and execute object store commands from the instance, just as you have just done from the undercloud now.

Ring files

Ring files are a kind of catalog of the files that are stored within the Swift storage engine and where within the storage cluster they are stored. As content is written to the Swift object storage cluster, these ring files are updated across the storage cluster and on the proxy server. When alternative storage backends are used in place of the Swift object storage engine, they mock the ring file system that the proxy expects and map this ring file system to its storage engine. Because the Swift proxy service always expects a set of ring files to operate, it is important to know how these are generated and installed. Learning how to set up ring files for the Swift object storage engine will teach you the basics that will translate into object storage backed by alternative storage engines.

There are various ring files that must all be generated and copied to each of the servers that will use the ring files. These include the account, container, and object rings. To generate these rings, each of the devices on each of the storage servers need to be added to the ring files, and the files need to be rebalanced before they are copied. In our example installation in *Chapter 1, RDO Installation*, Packstack did the setting up for us. This example is intended to give you an idea of how ring files are generated for future interactions you may have with generating these ring files.

Creating ring files

Let's use an example architecture that will include three storage nodes and one device on each of the nodes. If the IP addresses `192.168.123.11`, `192.168.123.12`, and `192.168.123.13` were the storage nodes and if each of them had a partition on a second drive named `sdb1`, then these three devices across the servers would be added to a new set of ring files using the `swift-ring-builder` command. First, create the ring files; this can be done on any of the storage nodes, and then the ring files will be copied to the other nodes. Here's how we use the `swift-ring-builder` command:

```
storage-node$ swift-ring-builder account.builder create 12 3 24

storage-node$ swift-ring-builder container.builder create 12 3 24

storage-node$ swift-ring-builder object.builder create 12 3 24
```

Here, you see a `create` command for each of the types of ring files. The three numbers behind the `create` command are the part power (`12`), replica count (`3`), and minimum part hours (`24`). There are partitions created within the Swift storage engine that help Swift to distribute the storage properly. The number of partitions is equal to 2 raised to the part power (`12`). In this example, 2^12 means that 4,096 partitions will be created in each ring. The replica count is how many copies of each item will be stored; it is recommended that you use three here. The minimum part hours is the minimum number of hours before a partition can be moved in succession. Swift recommends `24` as a good value for the minimum part hours. For more information on these values, search the Internet for *Swift preparing the rings* and you should find the official Swift documentation that goes into greater detail on how to choose values for these properties. Next, add the devices to the rings using the Swift ring builder command again. Here's how we go about it:

```
storage-node$ swift-ring-builder account.builder add z1-
192.168.123.11:6002/sdb1 100

storage-node$ swift-ring-builder account.builder add z1-
192.168.123.12:6002/sdb1 100

storage-node$ swift-ring-builder account.builder add z1-
192.168.123.13:6002/sdb1 100

storage-node$ swift-ring-builder account.builder rebalance

storage-node$ swift-ring-builder container.builder add z1-
192.168.123.11:6001/sdb1 100

storage-node$ swift-ring-builder container.builder add z1-
192.168.123.12:6001/sdb1 100

storage-node$ swift-ring-builder container.builder add z1-
192.168.123.13:6001/sdb1 100
```

```
storage-node$ swift-ring-builder container.builder rebalance

storage-node$ swift-ring-builder object.builder add z1-
192.168.123.11:6000/sdb1 100

storage-node$ swift-ring-builder object.builder add z1-
192.168.123.12:6000/sdb1 100

storage-node$ swift-ring-builder object.builder add
192.168.123.13:6000/sdb1 100

storage-node$ swift-ring-builder object.builder rebalance
```

In this example, there is only one zone used that is referenced by z1- as a prefix to each of the IP addresses. It is recommended that a minimum of five zones are used to avoid conflicts within zones on the same IP address. Behind each of the addresses and device names in these commands, there is a weight. This weight helps Swift to determine how many partitions are placed on the device relative to the rest of the devices in the cluster. It is recommended that you start with 100 times the number of terabytes on the drive. When this is complete, you should be able to list the files in your /etc/swift directory and see a .ring.gz file for each of the ring types. These are the files that need to be copied to each of the storage nodes and the Swift proxy server node before services are started. Also, ensure that these files on each of the nodes are owned by root:swift.

Once these files are in place across the servers, the services can be started. Note that Swift's configuration files do not reference the other servers in the storage cluster. The servers reference each other by way of ring files. These ring files can also be updated to help Swift work around hardware failures in the storage cluster. Just make sure that any changes that are made are copied across the cluster so that the ring files match on all the nodes.

Summary

In this chapter, we looked at using the Swift object storage and how to generate the ring files that the Swift storage engine uses to manage its storage. Now that we have covered the storage components in OpenStack, let's take a look at the Telemetry component that OpenStack uses to measure the usage of resources across the cluster.

8
Telemetry

Ceilometer is the telemetry component in OpenStack. While all the other components in OpenStack are busy managing virtual resources, Ceilometer keeps a watchful eye over them and measures the usage of resources, what resources are being used, and how they are being used within the cluster. In this chapter, we are going take a look at what is being measured and how to query the telemetry data. Then, we will use gnuplot to plot some of the data on a graph.

Understanding the data store

Before we start exploring Ceilometer, it is important to know that, by default, Ceilometer uses MongoDB to store all of its telemetry data. This data store can grow very rapidly and can use excess space. It is in your interest to keep Mongo's data store separate from the root partition of your control node so that the telemetry data does not fill up your control node's root disk. OpenStack has a horrible time functioning without a disk to write to. Mongo's data store is `/var/lib/mongodb/` by default. A simple way to be sure that the node's root disk doesn't fill up would be to mount another partition, logical volume, or some other external storage to `/var/lib/mongodb/`. If there isn't any important data in Ceilometer, you can even stop the MongoDB service, delete the contents of the data store directory, mount the new storage, ensure the ownership is correct, and restart the central and collector services of both the MongoDB and Ceilometer APIs. The files that were deleted will be recreated as an empty Mongo database for Ceilometer to start dumping data into again.

Definitions of Ceilometer's configuration terms

As resources are being managed within the OpenStack cluster, there are certain types of things that are being measured by Ceilometer. These types of things are called **meters** in Ceilometer. Each of these types of measurements gathers samples. Samples are single measurements or data points of a certain meter. The definition of how often to sample a meter is called a **pipeline**. Once enough samples are collected, they can be aggregated into statistics. Ceilometer statistics show a collection of samples over time for a particular meter. Ceilometer also has the ability to set alarms that will monitor statistics and is able to respond to matching criteria.

Pipelines

Pipelines are something that you shouldn't have to spend time configuring. Ceilometer has a collection of predefined pipelines that should suit most of your needs. If you end up needing a custom pipeline, it would be done in the `/etc/ceilometer/pipeline.yaml` configuration file. Take a look at this file if you would like to familiarize yourself with the pipeline configuration. We are not going to spend any more time beyond mentioning pipelines here.

Meters

Meters are the types of data being measured and the resources being measured. To see which meters have been collected and which resources have metered data, simply list the meters. Be sure to source your `overcloudrc` file first:

```
undercloud# ceilometer meter-list
```

Only meters that have collected data are included in this list. If a meter is absent, then there have not been any events to generate data for the absent meter. If no meters are listed, then the Ceilometer services are not properly collecting and reporting data. There is also a command that will show you which resources have collected telemetry data:

```
undercloud# ceilometer resource-list
```

After Ceilometer has been collecting data for an extended period of time, a very large `meter-list` could come back. This list can be filtered using the query argument:

```
undercloud# ceilometer meter-list -q name=vcpus
```

As a non-privileged user, you will only see meters for your project; as the administrator, you will probably need to filter the meters to a specific project. To do this, use the query argument to filter the list of meters:

```
undercloud# ceilometer meter-list -q project=<PROJECT_ID>
```

You can also pass multiple items to filter using a semicolon to delimit the filter items:

```
undercloud# ceilometer meter-list -q project=<PROJECT_ID>;name=vcpus
```

Samples

Now that you can retrieve the meters that are collecting data, you can look at what data has been collected for those meters. Samples are a single measurement of a meter for a resource. To get a list of samples, you will need to provide the meter that you would like to list samples for:

```
undercloud# ceilometer sample-list -m vcpus
```

As with the `meter-list` command, you can also filter the results with the query argument:

```
undercloud# ceilometer sample-list -m vcpus -q resource_id=<INSTANCE_ID>
```

You can also filter certain fields to get a range of results; for example, samples within a limited time period can be returned by filtering on the `timestamp` field:

```
undercloud# ceilometer sample-list -m vcpus -q
'resource_id=<INSTANCE_ID>;timestamp>2016-04-
27T07:30:00;timestamp<=2016-04-27T011:00:00'
```

Statistics

By listing the meters, we have looked at what is being measured, and by listing the samples, we have looked at the actual raw data that is being collected for the meters. The final aggregation of this data into something useful is called statistics in Ceilometer. As with samples, the `statistics` command requires you to provide the meter for which you would like to see statistics. Here's the `statistics` command:

```
undercloud# ceilometer statistics -m vcpus
```

As with meters and samples, a query argument can be passed to filter the data:

```
undercloud# ceilometer statistics -m vcpus -q 'timestamp>2016-04-
27T07:30:00;timestamp<=2016-04-27T011:00:00'
```

An additional argument that is available with `statistics` is the period argument. The period is the number of seconds into which samples can be grouped for the statistics generated. If you do not pass the period argument, you will get a single statistic returned to you with all the data for your meter and query. If you pass a period, you will get multiple statistics returned – one for each grouping of samples according to the period specified. For example, to get statistics for each 10-minute period within the timestamp range we have been using, the command would look like this:

```
undercloud# ceilometer statistics -m vcpus -q 'timestamp>2016-04-
27T07:30:00;timestamp<=2016-04-27T011:00:00' -p 600
```

Alarms

Alarms are a resource used mainly in conjunction with orchestration and autoscaling. We will look at alarms again when we look at orchestration in the next chapter. Alarms have to be created; they will not appear magically like the meters and samples we just looked at. Let's create an alarm that will watch for high CPU usage on a particular instance:

```
undercloud# ceilometer alarm-threshold-create --name cpu_alarm --
description 'cpu usage is high!' --meter-name cpu --threshold 80.0 --
comparison-operator gt  --statistic avg --period 600 --evaluation-
periods 3 --alarm-action 'log://' --query resource_id=<INSTANCE_ID>
```

This will create an alarm that watches the CPU on a specific instance and logs to the file if the instance's CPU usage is above 80 percent over three checks, 10 minutes apart. Use the `list` command to see the alarm just created:

```
undercloud# ceilometer alarm-list
```

Get the alarm's ID from the list and check its history:

```
undercloud# ceilometer alarm-history -a <ALARM_ID>
```

There is probably only a creation event; other events will show up in the history as they are triggered, though. Finally, it may be necessary to enable or disable the alarm for some reason. There is an `enabled` flag on alarms that you can use to turn it on and off:

```
undercloud# ceilometer alarm-update --enabled False -a <ALARM_ID>
```

Updates to the alarm using the `alarm-update` command are logged as history. After you have updated the alarm, look at the history again, and you will see an event for the update you made. This applies to any `alarm` property that is updated.

Graphing the data

Up until now, we have just seen data points flowing through our screen that may or may not be very useful to us. Wouldn't it be nice to make something visual to help display this data? There are plenty of options that could be used to plot this data. As an example, let's take a quick look at gnuplot, which is a command-line program that is packaged with most modern Linux distributions. This book has been using Fedora; to install gnuplot, simply `yum install` it:

```
undercloud# yum install -y gnuplot
```

There are options that need to be fed into `gnuplot` to tell it how to render the graph that it creates. Let's use a configuration file that will be passed to gnuplot. Put the following content into a file. I'm going to name mine `memory.cfg` because I will plot the memory usage that's already been aggregated by the Ceilometer `statistics` command:

```
#memory.conf
set terminal png truecolor
set output "memory.png"
set autoscale
set xdata time
set timefmt '%Y-%m-%dT%H:%M:%S'
set style data lines
plot '<cat' using 2:7 title "Sum"
```

The `set terminal` line tells gnuplot to generate a `.png` image. `Set output` sets the filename to write to. `Autoscale` turns on autoscaling. The `xdata` and `timefmt` lines define the format to read the time from. The `set style` line tells gnuplot to make a line graph. Finally, the plotline `<cat` reads from standard input. `2:7` tells us to use the second column for the *x* axis, the seventh column for the *y* axis, and the title `"Sum"` sets the title for the line that will be drawn. Next, let's execute the string of commands that will clean Ceilometer's output and give it to gnuplot:

```
undercloud# ceilometer statistics -m memory -q project=<PROJECT_ID> -p
3600 | tail -n +4 | head -n -1 | tr -d '|' | tr -s ' ' | gnuplot
memory.cfg
```

The Ceilometer `statistics` command uses the memory meter for the project of the ID that is passed and groups the memory measurements into hour-long periods. The Ceilometer output is piped to the tail, which strips off the rows that display the column headers. The `head` command strips off the last line, which is just another line as the one that was included in the header that borders the bottom of the data. The first `tr` command deletes all the pipes that are delimiting the columns, and the second `tr` command squashes all the spaces into single spaces. What we end up with is no pipe delimiting, no column headers, and no special output formatting. This is just the raw data with single-spaced delimiting. There may be a way to make Ceilometer do this automatically for us. Finally, the cleaned-up data is passed to gnuplot, which reads our configuration file and generates `.png`. Here is an image I generated with some sample data:

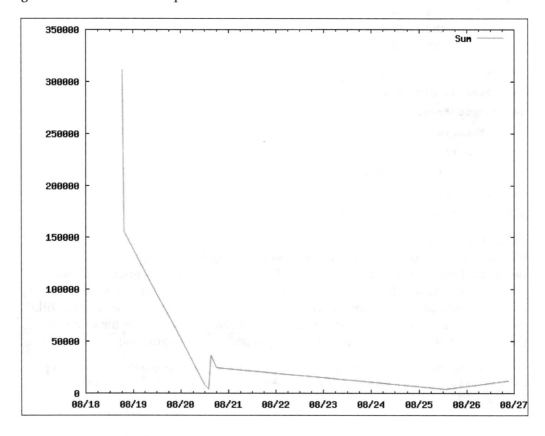

As a second example, let's plot two lines. This can't be achieved by piping data directly to gnuplot. We will have to dump the data into a data file so that the data can be read twice, once for each line. We will use vcpus this time instead of memory and a period of 30 minutes. Also, make a copy of the cfg file so that it can be modified:

```
undercloud# ceilometer statistics -m vcpus -q project=<PROJECT_ID> -p
1800 | tail -n +4 | head -n -1 | tr -d '|' | tr -s ' ' > vcpus.txt
undercloud# cp memory.cfg vcpus.cfg
```

Next, update the vcpus.cfg file to use the vcpus.txt file and to plot two lines instead of one. To do this, update the output line to a new filename so that you do not overwrite your memory.png file and update the plotline. The new file's content will look like this:

```
#vcpus.conf
set terminal png truecolor
set output "vcpus.png"
set autoscale
set xdata time
set timefmt '%Y-%m-%dT%H:%M:%S'
set style data lines
plot 'vcpus.txt' using 2:7 title "Sum", 'vcpus.txt' using 2:9
title "duration"
```

Once you have the new cfg file and the data file, run gnuplot:

```
undercloud# gnuplot vcpus.cfg
```

This will generate a `vcps.png` file. Here's one I generated with sample data:

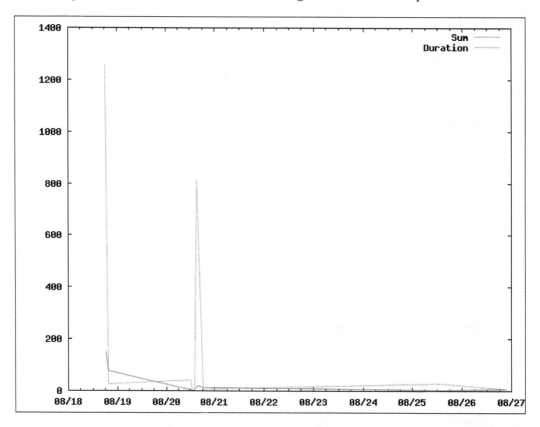

Another example that could be worked with is to dump the memory data into one file and have one line plotted from the memory data and the second line plotted from the vcpus data. As illustrated, gnuplot can be a powerful tool. These examples show what can be done with the data that Ceilometer produces. They show the only possible tool to consume and plot the data.

Summary

In this chapter, we looked at how to view, aggregate, and plot telemetry data using Ceilometer. This data is useful to monitor the health of a set of instances, a billing client, and so on. As mentioned in this chapter, Ceilometer's alarms are a useful resource for the orchestration tool in OpenStack. Next, we will look at cloud orchestration using the OpenStack component named Heat.

9
Orchestration

In the previous chapter, we looked at Ceilometer and used telemetry in OpenStack. In this chapter, we will take a look at orchestration using OpenStack's Heat component. We will take a look at what orchestration is and how to write a template for Heat. Then, we will use the template to launch a Heat stack.

About orchestration

In *Chapter 5*, *Instance Management*, we used Nova to launch instances in OpenStack. This example walked through launching a single instance or, if the instance count was increased, multiple instances with the same configuration. What if a collection of instances needed to be launched that required each of them to have a different configuration or they all needed to know about each other as part of their post-boot configuration? For example, maybe a different Glance image is needed for each instance or a different flavor is needed for the different roles within this collection of instances. It is even a possible requirement to control the order in which the instances are spawned to make sure that they are available in a specific order for post-boot configuration purposes. Enter orchestration. With OpenStack's orchestration component, Heat, all of these requirements and more can be met with Heat's capabilities.

Writing templates

The two core concepts to get started with Heat are stacks and templates. A stack is a collection of resources related to one another and launched by way of a template. A template is a text document definition of a stack. To launch a Heat stack, a Heat template is launched. Let's look at both of these in more depth, starting with templates.

Before we can launch a stack, we need a template that will define the stack. There are two template formats that you can use to launch a stack in Heat. One is the **AWS CloudFormation** template format. If you have ever used CloudFormation in **Amazon Web Services (AWS)**, then you will be familiar with this template format. Heat templates are very similar to those used within **AWS**, and add additional capabilities within OpenStack. The second format is the **Heat Orchestration Template (HOT)**. HOT is a native Heat template format that is written in the YAML Ain't Markup Language syntax. For more examples of both, visit the Heat-templates GitHub repository and browse through the collection of example scripts. The examples used in this chapter were pulled from `https://github.com/openstack/ heat-templates`.

The AWS CloudFormation format

Let's pull an example from the Heat-templates repository to gain some familiarity with the AWS CloudFormation format. Most of these templates are fairly large documents, so their entire contents will not be provided here. This document will be referenced from top to bottom. The document in its entirety is available at `https:// github.com/openstack/heat-templates/blob/master/cfn/F19/WordPress_ NoKey.yaml` and is also available in the code resources provided with this book.

Let's take a look at the configuration options used in this template:

- **HeatTemplateFormatVersion**: This is just for versioning so that Heat knows which syntax version is being used.

- **Description**: This is a description of what the template will launch. This template indicates it will launch a single-instance WordPress installation.

- **Parameters**: This is a section that defines what information is needed for this template to be launched. You can see that each of the parameters is defined by its name first and then a set of parameters to help the end user enter the correct information in it. For the template we are looking at, there are `InstanceType`, which references the flavors in Nova, and the `DBName`, `DBUsername`, `DBPassword`, and `DBRootPassword` properties that will be used to configure the database that will be created.

- **Mappings**: This template only maps flavors with images, so that when you launch a specific flavor, you will get the associated image.

- **Resources**: This section defines the resources that will be created in OpenStack. In this template, security group rules and an instance are created. You can see the security group rules to allow ICMP, port 80 (HTTP), and port 22 (SSH) traffic. You can also see the configuration options that will be passed to the instance when it is booted. These include packages to be installed, services to be started, the image to be used to launch the instance, which references the mappings we just looked at, the security group for the instance to reside in, and the user data that cloud-init should execute.

- **Outputs**: This section passes data back to Heat from the stack once it has been launched.

Next, let's take a look at the HOT format before we use a template to launch a stack.

The Heat Orchestration Template format

Take a look at the hello world template in the HOT directory in the same GitHub repository at `https://github.com/openstack/heat-templates/blob/master/hot/hello_world.yaml`.

The HOT format uses most of the same keywords that the AWS CloudFormation format uses. In the hello world template, you can see that almost all the same sections exist: `heat_template_version`, parameters, resources, and outputs. The configuration options for each of these sections look very similar; the main difference is that the HOT format is pure YAML and the AWS CloudFormation is a kind of YAML/JSON hybrid. The next step for us is to take these templates and launch a stack using them. We will use the HOT format to launch a stack next, so you will gain familiarity with this format in our practical application.

Launching a stack

Let's use the HOT hello world. The template can be passed to the Heat `stack-create` command as a local file, a URL to pull it from the network somewhere, or even as a Swift object if it was stored in Swift. It is important to validate a template. Pull down a copy of the template to your local filesystem.

Before you use this template, edit it and remove the constraints from `admin_pass`. It will make it easier to experiment with. Remove the lines under `admin_pass` that include constraints, length, and its description and both `allowed_pattern` and its description lines.

A template can be validated with Heat's `template-validate` command. Validating a template requires you to source a `keystonerc` file, use your `overcloudrc` file and then make sure that the template still validates with the changes you have made, as shown here:

```
undercloud# heat template-validate -f hello_world.yaml
```

Once the template validates, Heat will output a JSON representation of what it parsed from the template:

```
{
    "Description": "Hello world HOT template that just defines a single
server. Contains just base features to verify base HOT support.\n",
    "Parameters": {
      "admin_pass": {
        "Type": "String",
        "Description": "Admin password",
        "MinLength": 6,
        "Label": "admin_pass",
        "AllowedPattern": "[A-Z]+[a-zA-Z0-9]*",
        "NoEcho": "true",
        "MaxLength": 8,
        "ConstraintDescription": "Password length must be between 6 and
8 characters Password must consist of characters and numbers only
Password must start with an uppercase character"
      },
      "image": {
        "CustomConstraint": "glance.image",
        "Type": "String",
        "NoEcho": "false",
        "Description": "Image ID or image name to use for the server",
        "Label": "image"
      },
      "flavor": {
        "Description": "Flavor for the server to be created",
        "Default": "m1.small",
        "Label": "flavor",
        "CustomConstraint": "nova.flavor",
        "NoEcho": "false",
        "Type": "String"
      },
      "key_name": {
        "CustomConstraint": "nova.keypair",
        "Type": "String",
        "NoEcho": "false",
```

```
      "Description": "Name of an existing key pair to use for the
server",
      "Label": "key_name"
    },
    "db_port": {
      "Description": "Database port number",
      "Default": 50000,
      "Type": "Number",
      "MaxValue": 60000,
      "MinValue": 40000,
      "NoEcho": "false",
      "Label": "db_port",
      "ConstraintDescription": "Port number must be between 40000 and
60000"
    }
  }
}
```

Next, pass into the `stack-create` command a stack name and all the parameters that the template requires to launch:

```
undercloud# heat stack-create -f hello_world.yaml -P key_name=keypair_
name -P image=Fedora -P admin_pass=Abadpass my_first_stack
```

This command will launch a stack named `my_first_stack` from the template that you just downloaded. Once a stack has been launched, you can keep track of the stack's progress and details using Heat's `stack-list` command and the `stack-show` command. If there are nested stacks, add the `-show-nested` parameter to the `stack-list` command. This is useful when listing asking the undercloud for the overcloud heat stack, it has nested stacks as part of its deployment. Further, you can list the resources associated with the stack with the `resource-list` command, and you can see the individual resources through the other OpenStack components using the appropriate command associated with those resources. In this example, the only resource created was an instance through Nova, so use the `openstack server list` command to see the instance that the stack created. A stack also has a set of events. Those events can be listed with the `event-list` command. The details of resources and events can be seen with their respective `show` commands:

```
undercloud# heat stack-list
undercloud# heat stack-show {STACK_ID}
undercloud# heat resource-list {STACK_ID}
undercloud# heat resource-show {RESOURCE_ID}
undercloud# openstack server list
undercloud# heat event-list {STACK_ID}
undercloud# heat event-show {EVENT_ID}
```

Note here that the resources that are created through Heat can be managed independently of Heat. The instance that was created by way of the hello world stack could be deleted directly through Nova. Deleting the instance will not delete the stack, but deleting the stack will delete all the resources that are associated with the stack.

Autoscaling instances with Heat

Using Heat's autoscaling, it is possible to monitor a set of instances and add or subtract instances to meet load demands. In the same GitHub repository that the previous examples were taken from, there is an autoscaling example. For the autoscaling example to work, you will need to grab two templates:

- `https://github.com/openstack/heat-templates/blob/master/hot/autoscaling.yaml`

- `https://github.com/openstack/heat-templates/blob/master/hot/lb_server.yaml`

These templates are written to launch a single database instance and to add and remove web server instances respective to the load put on the WordPress stack running on the web servers.

LBaaS setup

Before we get to walking through these templates, we need to enable the **Load Balancer as a Service (LBaaS)** functionality of Neutron. Packstack does not configure it when it installs Neutron. There are a couple of configuration files to be updated and a couple of services to restart. First off, ensure that HAProxy is installed on the control node:

```
control# yum install -y haproxy
```

> Note that the contents of the file referenced in this chapter should not be replaced in their entirety. The configuration options listed are intended to be updated and the rest of the file left intact. If the contents of the files edited here include only the contents referenced here, then LBaaS will not be enabled properly, and this Heat template will fail to launch.

Next, edit `/etc/neutron/neutron.conf` on the control nodes and add the value `lbaas` to the `service_plugins` configuration option. If there are already values, leave them there and add `lbaas` to the comma-delimited list. Mine was commented out without a value, so I just added `lbaas` as the only value to this configuration. If yours is not commented, be sure to leave the plugins that are already listed. With only `lbass` enabled, it would look like this:

```
service_plugins = lbaas
```

With more than `lbass` enabled, it would be a comma-delimited list of plugins. Next, edit `/etc/neutron/lbaas_agent.ini` and make sure that the `device_driver` option is set to `HAProxy`, the `interface_driver` is set to `OVS` and that the `[haproxy]` `user_group` is set to `haproxy`:

```
[DEFAULT]
device_driver =
neutron.services.loadbalancer.drivers.haproxy.namespace_driver.Hap
roxyNSDriver
interface_driver = neutron.agent.linux.interface.OVSInterfaceDriver
[haproxy]
user_group = nobodyhaproxy
```

Finally, restart the Neutron server and `lbaas` services:

```
control# service neutron-servor restart
control# service neutron-lbaas-agent restart
```

Now that the `lbaas` service is enabled, let's take a look at the `autoscaling.yaml` file. This file was pulled from `https://github.com/openstack/heat-templates/blob/master/hot/autoscaling.yaml`. Here are the contents; there is more explanation after the contents of the file:

```
heat_template_version: 2013-05-23
description: AutoScaling Wordpress
parameters:
  image:
    type: string
    description: Image used for servers
  key:
    type: string
    description: SSH key to connect to the servers
  flavor:
    type: string
```

```
      description: flavor used by the web servers
    database_flavor:
      type: string
      description: flavor used by the db server
    network:
      type: string
      description: Network used by the server
    subnet_id:
      type: string
      description: subnet on which the load balancer will be located
    database_name:
      type: string
      description: Name of the wordpress DB
      default: wordpress
    database_user:
      type: string
      description: Name of the wordpress user
      default: wordpress
    external_network_id:
      type: string
      description: UUID of a Neutron external network
resources:
  database_password:
    type: OS::Heat::RandomString
  database_root_password:
    type: OS::Heat::RandomString
  db:
    type: OS::Nova::Server
    properties:
      flavor: {get_param: database_flavor}
      image: {get_param: image}
      key_name: {get_param: key}
      networks: [{network: {get_param: network} }]
      user_data_format: RAW
      user_data:
        str_replace:
          template: |
            #!/bin/bash -v
            yum -y install mariadb mariadb-server
            systemctl enable mariadb.service
            systemctl start mariadb.service
            mysqladmin -u root password $db_rootpassword
            cat << EOF | mysql -u root --password=$db_rootpassword
            CREATE DATABASE $db_name;
```

```
                    GRANT ALL PRIVILEGES ON $db_name.* TO "$db_user"@"%"
                    IDENTIFIED BY "$db_password";
                    FLUSH PRIVILEGES;
                    EXIT
                    EOF
                params:
                    $db_rootpassword: {get_attr: [database_root_password,
value]}
                    $db_name: {get_param: database_name}
                    $db_user: {get_param: database_user}
                    $db_password: {get_attr: [database_password, value]}
    asg:
      type: OS::Heat::AutoScalingGroup
      properties:
        min_size: 1
        max_size: 3
        resource:
          type: lb_server.yaml
          properties:
            flavor: {get_param: flavor}
            image: {get_param: image}
            key_name: {get_param: key}
            network: {get_param: network}
            pool_id: {get_resource: pool}
            metadata: {"metering.stack": {get_param: "OS::stack_id"}}
            user_data:
              str_replace:
                template: |
                  #!/bin/bash -v
                  yum -y install httpd wordpress
                  systemctl enable httpd.service
                  systemctl start httpd.service
                  setsebool -P httpd_can_network_connect_db=1

                  sed -i "/Deny from All/d" /etc/httpd/conf.d/wordpress.
conf
                  sed -i "s/Require local/Require all granted/" /etc/
httpd/conf.d/wordpress.conf
                  sed -i s/database_name_here/$db_name/ /etc/wordpress/
wp-config.php
                  sed -i s/username_here/$db_user/ /etc/wordpress/wp-
config.php
                  sed -i s/password_here/$db_password/ /etc/wordpress/
wp-config.php
```

```
                        sed -i s/localhost/$db_host/ /etc/wordpress/wp-config.
php

                        systemctl restart httpd.service
                params:
                    $db_name: {get_param: database_name}
                    $db_user: {get_param: database_user}
                    $db_password: {get_attr: [database_password, value]}
                    $db_host: {get_attr: [db, first_address]}
    web_server_scaleup_policy:
        type: OS::Heat::ScalingPolicy
        properties:
            adjustment_type: change_in_capacity
            auto_scaling_group_id: {get_resource: asg}
            cooldown: 60
            scaling_adjustment: 1
    web_server_scaledown_policy:
        type: OS::Heat::ScalingPolicy
        properties:
            adjustment_type: change_in_capacity
            auto_scaling_group_id: {get_resource: asg}
            cooldown: 60
            scaling_adjustment: -1
    cpu_alarm_high:
        type: OS::Ceilometer::Alarm
        properties:
            description: Scale-up if the average CPU > 50% for 1 minute
            meter_name: cpu_util
            statistic: avg
            period: 60
            evaluation_periods: 1
            threshold: 50
            alarm_actions:
                - {get_attr: [web_server_scaleup_policy, alarm_url]}
            matching_metadata: {'metadata.user_metadata.stack': {get_param:
"OS::stack_id"}}
            comparison_operator: gt
    cpu_alarm_low:
        type: OS::Ceilometer::Alarm
        properties:
            description: Scale-down if the average CPU < 15% for 10 minutes
            meter_name: cpu_util
            statistic: avg
            period: 600
```

```
            evaluation_periods: 1
            threshold: 15
            alarm_actions:
              - {get_attr: [web_server_scaledown_policy, alarm_url]}
            matching_metadata: {'metadata.user_metadata.stack': {get_param:
"OS::stack_id"}}
            comparison_operator: lt
      monitor:
        type: OS::Neutron::HealthMonitor
        properties:
          type: TCP
          delay: 5
          max_retries: 5
          timeout: 5
      pool:
        type: OS::Neutron::Pool
        properties:
          protocol: HTTP
          monitors: [{get_resource: monitor}]
          subnet_id: {get_param: subnet_id}
          lb_method: ROUND_ROBIN
          vip:
            protocol_port: 80
      lb:
        type: OS::Neutron::LoadBalancer
        properties:
          protocol_port: 80
          pool_id: {get_resource: pool}

      # assign a floating ip address to the load balancer
      # pool.
      lb_floating:
        type: OS::Neutron::FloatingIP
        properties:
          floating_network_id: {get_param: external_network_id}
          port_id: {get_attr: [pool, vip, port_id]}

outputs:
  scale_up_url:
    description: >
      This URL is the webhook to scale up the autoscaling group.  You
      can invoke the scale-up operation by doing an HTTP POST to this
      URL; no body nor extra headers are needed.
```

```
        value: {get_attr: [web_server_scaleup_policy, alarm_url]}
  scale_dn_url:
    description: >
      This URL is the webhook to scale down the autoscaling group.
      You can invoke the scale-down operation by doing an HTTP POST to
      this URL; no body nor extra headers are needed.
    value: {get_attr: [web_server_scaledown_policy, alarm_url]}
  pool_ip_address:
    value: {get_attr: [pool, vip, address]}
    description: The IP address of the load balancing pool
  website_url:
    value:
      str_replace:
        template: http://host/wordpress/
        params:
          host: { get_attr: [lb_floating, floating_ip_address] }
    description: >
      This URL is the "external" URL that can be used to access the
      Wordpress site.
  ceilometer_query:
    value:
      str_replace:
        template: >
          ceilometer statistics -m cpu_util
          -q metadata.user_metadata.stack=stackval -p 600 -a avg
        params:
          stackval: { get_param: "OS::stack_id" }
    description: >
      This is a Ceilometer query for statistics on the cpu_util meter
      Samples about OS::Nova::Server instances in this stack.  The -q
      parameter selects Samples according to the subject's metadata.
      When a VM's metadata includes an item of the form metering.X=Y,
      the corresponding Ceilometer resource has a metadata item of the
      form user_metadata.X=Y and samples about resources so tagged can
      be queried with a Ceilometer query term of the form
      metadata.user_metadata.X=Y.  In this case the nested stacks give
      their VMs metadata that is passed as a nested stack parameter,
      and this stack passes a metadata of the form metering.stack=Y,
      where Y is this stack's ID.
```

You will see that the parameters collect the information necessary to dynamically launch the instances, attach them to networks, and create a database name and user to set up the database. The first three resources in the resource definitions include the database server itself and randomly generated passwords for the database users. The next resource is an autoscaling group. The group is of the `AutoScalingGroup` type, and the resource defined in this group is of the `lb_server.yaml` type. This refers to the other YAML file available from `https://github.com/openstack/heat-templates/blob/master/hot/lb_server.yaml`. Let's quickly look at this template:

```
heat_template_version: 2013-05-23
description: A load-balancer server
parameters:
  image:
    type: string
    description: Image used for servers
  key_name:
    type: string
    description: SSH key to connect to the servers
  flavor:
    type: string
    description: flavor used by the servers
  pool_id:
    type: string
    description: Pool to contact
  user_data:
    type: string
    description: Server user_data
  metadata:
    type: json
  network:
    type: string
    description: Network used by the server

resources:
  server:
    type: OS::Nova::Server
    properties:
      flavor: {get_param: flavor}
      image: {get_param: image}
      key_name: {get_param: key_name}
      metadata: {get_param: metadata}
      user_data: {get_param: user_data}
      user_data_format: RAW
      networks: [{network: {get_param: network} }]
```

```
    member:
      type: OS::Neutron::PoolMember
      properties:
        pool_id: {get_param: pool_id}
        address: {get_attr: [server, first_address]}
        protocol_port: 80

  outputs:
    server_ip:
      description: IP Address of the load-balanced server.
      value: { get_attr: [server, first_address] }
    lb_member:
      description: LB member details.
      value: { get_attr: [member, show] }
```

The `lb_server.yaml` template is a fairly basic server definition to launch a single instance using Heat. The extra definitions to note are the `pool_id` parameter and the `Neutron PoolMember` resource. These associate the servers that are launched with this template with the LBaaS pool resource created in the `autoscaling.yaml` template. This also shows an example of how Heat templates can reference each other. Let's jump back to the `autoscaling.yaml` template now.

The next two resources defined after the `AutoScalingGroup` resource are the Heat policies that are used to define what to do when scaling up or scaling down. The next two resources are the Ceilometer alarms that trigger the Heat policies to scale up or down accordingly when the CPU usage is too high or too low for the number of instances that are currently running. The last four resources define a load balancer, an IP address for the load balancer, a monitor for the load balancer, and a pool to add servers to for the load balancer to balance the load.

Lastly, the `autoscale.yaml` template defines a set of outputs to get URLs and the pool IP address or that the heat stack can be used.

Now that we've walked through these templates, let's launch the autoscale template. You will need to pass in a Glance image ID to launch all the instances off, the ID of your internal subnet and your external network, a key pair's name, and Nova flavor names for the database and the web server instances. The `stack-create` command should be executed as the admin user. The policies in Ceilometer require admin access. They could be created ahead of time and provided to end users if it was necessary for non-administrative users to launch autoscaling stacks. For our demonstrations here, just use the admin user. The command will look something like this:

```
heat stack-create -f autoscaling.yaml -P database_flavor=m1.small -P
subnet_id={INTERNAL_SUBNET_ID} -P external_network_id={EXT_NET_ID} -P
image={GLANCE_IMAGE_ID} -P key=danradez -P flavor=m1.small autoscale_me
```

Once the stack launches, you can use the stack, resource, and event commands to list and show information about the stack, monitor its progress, and troubleshoot any errors that might be encountered. This stack is now ready to scale automatically using the resources Heat has put into place to monitor the set of resources created through this stack. If you were to put a load on the web service instance enough to trigger the scale-up alarm, another instance would spawn. You can also accomplish this via POST to the scale-up URL listed in the outputs of the autoscaling template. Similarly, reducing the load to trigger the scale-down alarm or a POST to the scale-down URL in the outputs section of the template would reduce the number of instances in the web server pool.

Web interface

Now that we have looked at Heat on the command line and explored some of its functionality, let's take a look at the dashboard and the support available for Heat in the dashboard web interface. Log in to the dashboard, find the **Orchestration** menu, and select the **Stacks** menu option. The following screenshot captures the dashboard:

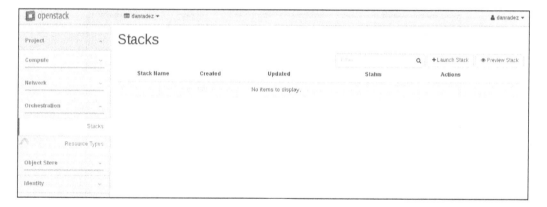

To launch a new stack, click on the **Launch Stack** button in the top-right corner:

To launch your stack, you have the same options to pull your template from. I have chosen the same `hello_world.yaml` file used earlier:

Fill out the form to provide the parameters required to launch the stack. Then, click on the **Launch** button at the bottom of the form. You may have to scroll down to get to it. If the form validation fails, you will be notified as to what needs to be updated:

The web interface will auto-update itself until the stack reaches a complete or failed state. Click on the **Stack Name** to drill down and find out more information about the stack. There are tabs with identification details, a **Resources** list, and an **Event** list. One other tab available is the **Topology** tab. This tab is more interesting with more resources; the hello world stack only has one item on it. Here's what the topology looked like after I launched the autoscaling template:

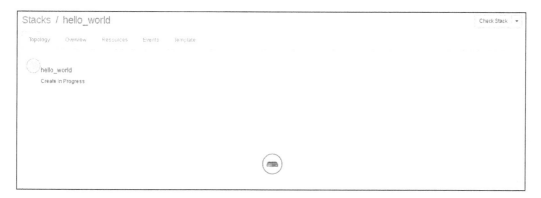

Each of the circles can be moused over to show what each of them are and what their status is. Their status also shows failure reasons, so if something fails, this is sometimes a convenient place to get a visual representation of what failed and what the error message from the failure is. The graph is also interactive in a drag-around kind of way, which makes for great eye candy.

Summary

In this chapter, we looked at the different kinds of Heat templates and how to launch Heat stacks from these templates. Heat stacks offer a new level of opportunity to launch instances and tie them all together into a useful and functional set of instances and complementary resources. This completes the set of OpenStack components that we are going to review in this book.

In the upcoming chapters, we are going to look at how to architect an OpenStack cluster, how to monitor the cluster, and how to troubleshoot OpenStack infrastructure. In the next chapter, we will integrate Docker container support into your OpenStack cluster. OpenStack can be an effective method to managing Docker containers.

Next, you will get you get a taste of getting started with Docker containers in OpenStack.

10
Docker

In the previous chapters, we have looked at the components that are used to launch virtual instances in OpenStack. These instances have been targeting the end result of virtual machines running on the compute nodes. Containers have become a very popular alternative to virtual machines for certain workloads. In this chapter, we will work through the configuration changes that are required to deploy Docker containers using OpenStack.

Containers

A container shares the kernel and system resources of its host. This is different from a virtual machine because a virtual machine has its own kernel and related resources. Containers do have their own filesystem tree. A very basic use of containers is to separate applications and runtimes from each other. There are more advanced uses that we are not able to explore here. What is important here is that OpenStack can be used to manage these containers. Containers are more lightweight than virtual machines but still provide a level of isolation for deployments. These can be managed, conceptually, very much like a virtual machine.

OpenStack integration

To integrate Docker with OpenStack, a compute node's driver needs to be changed from `libvirt` to `docker`. This forces an entire compute node's worth of virtualization capacity to be converted to container capacity. Docker containers and virtual machines cannot coexist on a compute node together. Docker containers and virtual machines can coexist in the same OpenStack cluster as long as there are at least two compute nodes, one for containers and one for virtual machines. For now, you will convert your existing compute node to `docker`, then in *Chapter 11*, *Scaling Horizontally*, you will attach another compute node to re-enable virtual machine management.

Nova compute configuration

To configure a compute node to use Docker, there is a Docker driver that needs to be installed on the compute node to use as the compute Nova compute's driver. There are directions for how to do everything, which we will discuss in the documentation in the GitHub repository for the `nova-docker` driver at `https://github.com/openstack/nova-docker`.

The first task is to delete the virtual machines running. Once the following configuration is completed, OpenStack will not be able to manage the virtual machines running on the compute node. Go ahead and delete any running instances you have.

Next, let's walk through the setup instructions. Start by logging into a compute node, installing `git`, `docker`, and Docker Python support, cloning the `nova-docker` GitHub repository, and running `setup.py` to install the driver:

```
compute# yum install -y git docker python-docker-py
compute# systemctl enable docker
compute# git clone https://github.com/openstack/nova-docker
compute# cd nova-docker
compute# python setup.py install
```

Now that the `nova-docker` driver is installed, modify the configuration file `/etc/nova/nova.conf`. Update the `compute_driver` setting from the `libvirt` driver to the `docker` driver. The `compute_driver` parameter will be commented out. Add another line below it with the new value. That way, you know what the default value was and the new value will be active:

```
#compute_driver=libvirt.LibvirtDriver
compute_driver=novadocker.virt.docker.DockerDriver
```

For these changes to take effect, restart the Nova compute service. The `docker` driver will try to connect to the `docker` service, so start `docker` first:

```
compute# systemctl start docker
compute# systemctl restart openstack-nova-compute
```

Glance configuration

When Docker boots a container, it will need to start the container from a Docker image, similar to how it needs to start a virtual machine from a disk image. Nova will need to pull this container from Glance. This means that Glance needs to know how to manage Docker containers. In Mitaka, Glance knows how to handle Docker containers by default. This can be confirmed by looking in the `/etc/glance/glance-api.conf` file and verifying that `docker` is listed in the `container_formats` list. Note that container of `container_formats` here does not refer to a `docker` container. It is related to the storage capabilities that Glance has.

Importing a Docker image to Glance

Now that it has been confirmed that Glance can manage the Docker container, one must be imported into Glance and made available to boot a container instance. To do this, you use Docker to get images and then import them into Glance so they are available to Nova at spawn time for the instance. Docker needs to be installed and running on the host you do this from and you must execute the OpenStack command-line client. Let's do this work on the undercloud since that is where you have been sourcing the `overcloudrc` file. Start by making sure that Docker is installed and running:

```
undercloud$ sudo yum install docker -y
undercloud$ sudo systemctl start docker
undercloud$ sudo systemctl enable docker
```

Next, use Docker to download the CentOS Docker image. This will have to be done as the root user as permissions have not been set up for non-root users to connect to the `docker` daemon. The `pull` command will copy the Docker image into Docker's image store. You can see the downloaded image using the Docker `images` command:

```
undercloud$ sudo docker pull centos
undercloud$ sudo docker images
```

Finally, export the Docker image using Docker's `save` command and pipe the data to the OpenStack's `image create` command:

```
undercloud$ source overcloudrc
undercloud$ sudo docker save centos | openstack image create centos
--public --container-format docker --disk-format raw
```

It is important to name the Glance image the same as it is named in the Docker image list. If these names do not match then the Docker image will not be referenced properly and glance will not be able to properly provide the image to nova when the instance boots.

Also, pay attention to the permissions that these commands run with. The `docker` command is running `sudo` to connect to the `docker` daemon and the data is being piped to the `openstack` command that is no longer being run as root. The `openstack` command is connecting to OpenStack using the admin user's credentials. You should only load Docker images into OpenStack using the admin user.

Using the OpenStack's `image list` command, you will see the CentOS image that you imported. Doing an `image show` on the instance node that the container-format has been specified as `docker`:

```
undercloud$ openstack image list
undercloud$ openstack image show docker-centos
```

Launching a Docker instance

Now that a there is a compute node that is configured to use the `docker` driver and there is a Glance image available to launch from, you are ready to boot a Docker container with OpenStack. The docker integration that you have completed enables a Docker instance to be launched the same way that a virtual machine instance is launched:

```
undercloud# openstack server create --flavor 1 --image centos --key-name
openstack --nic net-id={internal net-id} "My First Docker Instance"
```

The container will be spawned on the compute node that supports Docker and will become active. Once it is active, there is the question of what to do with it? Generally, a container is launched with intent to run a specific process. As an example, we can tell the Docker image to run the SSH daemon on boot as its process. Doing this, it can be connected to over SSH similar to a virtual machine:

```
undercloud# glance image-update --property os_command_line='/usr/sbin/
sshd -D' centos
undercloud# openstack server create --flavor 1 --image centos --key-name
openstack --nic net-id={internal net-id} "My SSH Docker Instance"
```

Once the new Docker instance becomes active, you use OpenStack server list to get the list of instances and use the IP address assigned to the Docker instances to SSH to it.

Summary

In this chapter, we have explored the integration of Docker into an OpenStack cluster. In a cluster that has multiple compute nodes, Docker instances and virtual machine instances can coexist with one another. Remember that they cannot co-exist on the same compute node. A single compute node is dedicated to either virtual machines or to Docker containers.

In *Chapter 11*, *Scaling Horizontally*, we will add a second compute node to re-enable your OpenStack deployment to have virtual machine capability. Once the new node is added, you will have the capability to run both Docker containers and virtual machines in your OpenStack cluster.

11
Scaling Horizontally

One of the foundations of OpenStack is that it was built to run on generic commodity hardware and is intended to scale out horizontally very easily. Scaling horizontally means adding more commodity servers to get the job done. Scaling vertically means getting larger, more specialized servers. Whether the servers you run have a handful of processors and a few gigabytes of RAM, or double digits of processors and RAM approaching or exceeding terabytes, OpenStack will run on your servers. Further, whatever assortment of servers of varying horsepower you have collected, they can all be joined into an OpenStack cluster to run the API services, service agents, and hypervisors within the cluster. The only hard requirement is that your processors have virtualization extensions built into them, which is pretty much a standard feature in most modern-day processors. In this chapter, we will look at the process of scaling an OpenStack cluster horizontally on the control and compute layers. Then, we will discuss the concepts around making the cluster highly available.

Scaling compute nodes

The first and easiest way to scale an OpenStack cluster is to add compute power. One control node can support more than one compute node. Remember installing RDO in *Chapter 1, RDO Installation*? We have come a long way since then! In that example, only one compute node was installed. One control node can support a large collection of compute nodes. The exact number that can be handled depends on the demand put on the cluster by its end users. It is probably safe to say that the capacity provided by one compute node is probably not going to meet most use cases, so let's take a look at how to add additional compute nodes to our OpenStack installation.

There are only two OpenStack services, NTP, and the supporting networking infrastructure that a new compute node needs to be running for it to be joined into an OpenStack cluster and start sharing the computing workload. These two services are the Nova compute service and the Neutron Open vSwitch agent. In our example installation, the supporting networking infrastructure is Open vSwitch, so Open vSwitch is required in this example. The Ceilometer compute agent can also optionally be installed if the telemetry data is expected to be collected. As soon as the Nova and Neutron agents communicate with the control tier, the node will be available for new instances to be scheduled as long as everything is properly configured.

Enter the great configuration complexity of OpenStack. A configuration management engine will make this process much simpler. There are a handful of configuration management engines out there that have a vibrant community and an active investment in a set of maintained modules that can be used to install and configure OpenStack. In *Chapter 1, RDO Installation*, Triple-O was used to install the OpenStack overcloud. Under the hood, Triple-O uses the configuration management engine puppet to do the heavy lifting of installation and configuration. Triple-O offers the facility to make additions and modifications to the original deployment by reusing the original deployment command. Before we use Triple-O to add another node, let's see the compute node already associated with our OpenStack cluster and what its status is using OpenStack's hypervisor commands:

```
undercloud# source overcloudrc
undercloud# openstack hypervisor list
undercloud# openstack hypervisor show 1
```

This command will output a list of the hypervisors registered with OpenStack. Pass the hypervisor's ID to the show command and look for the state and uptime fields. These will indicate if the node is healthy or not. Next, let's go ahead and add a new compute node to the cluster.

If you remember the installation from *Chapter 1, RDO Installation*, a configuration file was passed to the Triple-O quickstart. This configuration file was populated with a list of nodes that could be used with a quickstart deployment. To add a second compute node, it is as simple as rerunning the overcloud deploy command and indicating to use the second compute node:

```
undercloud# source stackrc
undercloud# openstack overcloud deploy --control-scale 1 --compute-scale
2 --templates --libvirt-type qemu --ceph-storage-scale 1 -e /usr/share/
openstack-tripleo-heat-templates/environments/storage-environment.yaml
```

Notice that compute-scale has been increased from 1 to 2. Triple-O will try to run puppet on both defined compute nodes. The puppet run on the existing compute node will net no new changes. The second compute node will be booted, configured, and joined to the overcloud. It is important to understand that when the `quickstart.sh` file created these virtual machines to represent the bare-metal nodes, it also created a definition file that was imported into the undercloud. This is the `instackenv.json` file that is in the stack user's home directory on the undercloud. Open this file and inspect it to see the same list of nodes that were originally added to the `openstac_essentials.yml` file, except with information that defines how to manage their power state. If you need to add additional nodes, for instance, if you are managing baremetal compute nodes, the process of running overcloud deployment is the same. Just increase the `compute-scale`, `control-scale` or `ceph-scale` parameter accordingly. The difference is that the new nodes need to be defined and imported into the undercloud the same way that the original `instackenv.json` file was imported in *Chapter 1, RDO Installation*. The new node definitions can be added directly to the original `instackenv.json` file and re-imported with the same command used in *Chapter 1, RDO Installation*. To see the list of available nodes for Triple-O to use, run OpenStack's `baremetal` command:

```
undercloud# openstack baremetal list
```

Nodes in this list will be in a provisioning state `available` and have no instance ID associated with them when they can be used to deploy new overcloud nodes to them. If there is an instance ID, the nodes are already allocated and cannot be used to add new nodes to the overcloud.

When the overcloud deploy running to add the second compute node finishes, look at the list of hypervisors again and you will see the second hypervisor joined into the overcloud:

```
undercloud# source overcloudrc
undercloud# openstack hypervisor list
```

This process can be repeated for more compute nodes as long as there are `baremetal` nodes available in the `baremetal` node list. As more nodes are added as compute nodes, the Nova scheduler will spawn instances across all the nodes according to its scheduling algorithm.

Installing more control nodes

Adding more control nodes adds more complexity than adding compute nodes. Generally, when additional control nodes are added, each of the control services need to be scaled and the database and message bus need to become highly available.

Triple-O has the capability to install and configure highly available scaled services for you. There is a wealth of documentation on OpenStack's Triple-O Wiki at `http://docs.openstack.org/developer/tripleo-docs/`. Be sure to take a look at the documentation there if you are trying to deploy something that has not been covered in this book.

As long as there are `bare-metal` nodes available, just a few extra parameters need to be added to the overcloud deploy command to deploy a multi-control node deployment. It is not recommended to update an existing control tier. It is recommended to plan ahead accordingly and deploy all the control nodes for the first using these parameters. Here is an example of a deployment that would have three control nodes, three compute nodes and three `ceph` nodes. Three control nodes is the minimum number of control nodes in a multi-control node deployment. More information on why three control nodes is the minimum in the *High availability* section coming up:

```
undercloud# openstack overcloud deploy --control-scale 3 --compute-
scale 3 --templates --libvirt-type qemu --ceph-storage-scale 3 -e /usr/
share/openstack-tripleo-heat-templates/environments/storage-environment.
yaml -e /usr/share/openstack-tripleo-heat-templates/environments/puppet-
pacemaker.yaml --ntp-server pool.ntp.org
```

The addition to this command includes the increased number of each type of node, the `puppet-pacemaker.yaml` file and the `ntp-server`. Let's take a brief look in more detail at what will be added by the additional configuration parameters.

Load-balancing control services

When more compute services are added to the cluster, OpenStack's scheduler distributes the new instances appropriately. When new control or network services are added, traffic has to be deliberately sent to them. There is not anything natively in OpenStack that handles traffic being distributed across the API services. There is a load-balancing service called **HAProxy** that can do this for us. HAProxy can be run anywhere it can access the endpoints that will be balanced. It could go on its own node or it could be put on a node that already has a bit of OpenStack installed on it. Triple-O will run HAProxy on each of the control nodes.

HAProxy has a concept of frontends and backends. The frontends are where HAProxy listens for incoming traffic, and the backends define where the incoming traffic will be sent to and balanced across. When a user makes an API call to one of the OpenStack services, the HAProxy frontend assigned to the service will receive the request. HAProxy will make a decision about which backend should receive the traffic. There will be one backend configured for each control node. This is because the service should be running on each of the control nodes. The backend has no knowledge of HAProxy and is serving traffic as if it was being called directly by the end user. The frontend and backend definitions are configured in /etc/haproxy/ haproxy.cfg. Have a look at this file if you are interested in learning more about HAProxy's configuration.

The control services can be load-balanced like this because they are stateless applications. This means that no information is associated across multiple requests. Each time a user makes a request to an OpenStack API endpoint, their authentication token is validated, the request is processed, and the request is terminated.

High availability

While HAProxy has monitors built into it to check the health of a host, this is only to know whether or not to send traffic to the host. It does not include any capability of recovering from failure.

To make the control tier highly available, **Pacemaker** is added to the cluster to monitor services, filesystems, networking resources, and other resources that is it not sufficient to simply load-balance, they need to be made highly available. Pacemaker is capable of moving services from node to node in a pacemaker cluster and monitoring the nodes to know whether action needs to be taken to recover a particular resource or even one of the entire nodes. Triple-O will install and configure a highly available control tier with the previously shown options passed to overcloud deploy in this chapter.

There are two major infrastructure considerations that go into designing a Pacemaker cluster. These points are related to the installation of Pacemaker and preparing it to start managing resources that you would like to be highly available. First, at least three nodes are needed to properly configure Pacemaker and establish a quorum. With only two nodes, if communication is lost between them, they can enter a state called **split brain**. This is when the nodes both think that they should be the primary node because they cannot reach the other node. In this case, resources that should only reside on one server can be started in two places and cause conflict, for example, the **Virtual IPs (VIPs)**. We will discuss the VIPs a little more in just a moment. When there are more than two nodes, there will be a vote cast from the nodes before an action takes place. For example, if one node loses communication with the other, two or more nodes will have to vote for that node to be fenced. When the majority agrees on the action, then the power to the node is cut to reboot it.

Second, fencing must be configured for a proper Pacemaker installation. Fencing is the capability of nodes within the cluster to control the power of each other. In the event that one node loses communication with the others, the other nodes must be able to do something about it. Without the ability to communicate with one of the nodes, the other nodes will first agree that they all cannot communicate with it, then it will be fenced. To fence a node, the power to it is cut to power-cycle it and to force it to reboot in the hope that a fresh boot will restore its communication with the cluster.

Once a Pacemaker cluster is set up and running, it will be ready to have resources configured within it to be highly available. An example set of resources that should be made highly available are HAProxy and the VIP that it is listening in on. HAProxy is a single point of failure for all of the API traffic being passed through it. By adding it as a resource to Pacemaker, it will be monitored to ensure that the IP address is always reachable on one of Pacemaker's nodes and that HAProxy is listening in on that IP address to receive incoming traffic. VIPs are not persisted across boots on the control node. That is because when they are added to Pacemaker as a resource, Pacemaker will handle the configuration and health of that IP address for you.

Almost all of the other OpenStack services can be made highly available. Most of them can be added to Pacemaker in what is called a **cloned configuration**. That means that Pacemaker expects to run them on more than one node but will monitor their health and restart them if they go down. This is the configuration Triple-O will use the services that are being load-balanced by HAProxy.

Highly available database and message bus

The database and the message bus are not necessarily OpenStack services, but they are services that OpenStack depends on and that you want to be sure are highly available too. One option to make the database highly available is to add it to Pacemaker with a shared storage device. If the database were to fail on a node, then Pacemaker would move the shared storage to another node and start the database on a different node. There are also active/passive and active/active replication scenarios that can be configured for the database. Active/passive means that there is more than one instance of the database running, but only one of them is used as the active writable instance. The other instance(s) are there as passive backups and only become active if the current active instance needs to fail over for some reason. Active/active means that there is more than one active writable instance of the database. These are running on different nodes and each can be read from and written to as equal members of the database cluster. Replication is important in both of these scenarios because the database cannot read and write to the same data store at the same time. To overcome this, databases can be configured to replicate their data so that each instance has its own datastore and so that transactions in the database are duplicated to each of the database instances to preserve the integrity of the data in the database.

The message bus is in a similar situation, the main difference being that it does not have a persistent data store such as a database. It can be configured in a pure failover mode where it would only run on one node, an active/passive configuration, or an active/active configuration. Each of these configurations has its positives and negatives and should be researched in more depth before one is chosen for implementation. The primary concern with a message bus is making sure that two different nodes do not process the same message so that it does not get duplicated within the message bus and cause one action to happen twice.

Summary

In this chapter, we looked at the concepts involved in scaling and load-balancing OpenStack services. We have also touched upon the concepts involved in making OpenStack highly available. Now that an OpenStack cluster is up and running and we have discussed how it could be scaled to meet demand, in the next chapter, we are going to take a look at monitoring the cluster to keep track of its health and help diagnose trouble when it arises.

12
Monitoring

As an OpenStack cluster is scaled out, the number of moving parts that can get jammed increases. As you have seen, each server added to the cluster will run more than one service. Each of those services interacts and communicates with each other across the cluster, using different communication methods and unique endpoints for each service. This presents a complicated web of interdependence that can be very complicated to debug when something goes wrong. Monitoring all the moving parts can save a large amount of time and hassle in trying to figure out what has gone wrong when things stop working.

In this chapter, we will look at setting up monitoring for the cluster to help you have a detailed view of the general health of a running OpenStack cluster.

Monitoring defined

There are two classifications of monitoring, performance monitoring and availability monitoring. Performance monitoring shows the performance of what is being monitored over time. Availability monitoring show the status of what is being monitored at a point in time. Often, the same things are monitored, but the purposes of the two types of monitoring are different. As an example, if a server's CPU utilization was being monitored, availability monitoring checks the CPU utilization, and if it breaches a certain threshold, the monitoring alerts an operator that the utilization is high or may have remained high over the most recent checks. Performance monitoring keeps track of the CPU utilization in the longer term and most likely creates a graph to show the trend of CPU utilization on a server across days or weeks or longer.

In this chapter, we will focus on availability monitoring to be able to determine the current health of an OpenStack cluster based on the current status of the checks being run on the servers in the cluster.

Installing Nagios

Nagios is an open source monitoring tool that is well known and widely accepted by system administrators. There are other OpenSource options available as well, such as Zabbix or Sensu. We won't be able to get into those here. Just know that they are available and can help your monitoring needs.

There are plans in the works for monitoring installation to be added to a Triple-O deployment. Keep watch on the community for progress that is made on this. For now, we will install Nagios and look at what configurations can be dropped in to monitor an OpenStack installation. Start by installing Nagios, setting it to start on boot and starting the service:

```
undercloud# sudo yum install nagios nagios-plugins-all nagios-plugins-
nrpe -y
undercloud# sudo chkconfig nagios on
undercloud# sudo systemctl start nagios
```

When `nagios` is installed, it adds configuration to Apache to serve a web page for you to see the status. Open `http://192.0.2.1/nagios/` in a web browser. The default username and password for the web page is `nagiosadmin/nagiosadmin`. When the web page is opened, there will be two links of interest. On the left-hand side of the screen, there will be a hosts and a services link. You will see that there is a default localhost configuration that is installed for you. The configuration for localhost is defined in `/etc/nagios/objects/localhost.cfg`. The `plugins-all` package that was installed with Nagios provides the plugins that are necessary for the localhost service checks to pass.

The localhost file could be copied and updated appropriately for each host that you would like to monitor if you want a base set of checks for a host. Servers that are included in an OpenStack cluster need more specific monitoring. Let's add configurations to the Nagios configuration files to monitor the OpenStack hosts and services. To apply configuration changes, the service will need to be restarted for Nagios to read the updates and start checks based on the new configurations. For example, we will refer to a set of monolithic configuration files to configure Nagios in this chapter. Each file that is referred to in this chapter will be placed in the drop directory `/etc/nagios/conf.d`. The top-level Nagios configuration file `/etc/nagios/nagios.cfg` includes files placed in this directory. There are options to break up the files referenced in this chapter; the way that the localhost file is structured is one example. It is beyond the scope of this chapter to go further into splitting the configuration files. Please search for documentation on this if you choose to split up your configuration files further.

Adding Nagios host checks

Start by adding host checks. The first example's configuration file will hold all the configuration stanzas for the hosts in the cluster that we are going to monitor. Let's use the file /etc/nagios/conf.d/nagios_host.cfg. This establishes a check to ensure that each host is up and responding to network communication. If you have additional compute nodes, make sure to add them as well. Here's the configuration that would cover the control, two compute and the ceph nodes. Be sure to use OpenStack server list to get the correct IP addresses and hostnames:

```
define host {
address 192.0.2.9
host_name overcloud-controller-0
use linux-server
}
define host {
address 192.0.2.10
host_name overcloud-novacompute-0
use linux-server
}
define host {
address 192.0.2.11
host_name overcloud-novacompute-1
use linux-server
}
define host {
address 192.0.2.8
host_name overcloud-cephstorage-0
use linux-server
}
```

After adding these configurations, validate the Nagios configuration and restart the Nagios service:

```
$ service nagios configcheck
Running configuration check... OK.
$ service nagios restart
```

Often a configuration gets a fat-finger error in it and the configuration validation will fail. When that happens, Nagios will fail to start. To find out where the syntax error is, run Nagios by hand by referencing the top-level configuration file:

```
$ nagios -v /etc/nagios/nagios.cfg
```

This will give you the line that the syntax error is on. If Nagios restarts successfully, you should be able to connect to Nagios on port 80, select the host list, and after some time passes and the checks fire, a health check will succeed on your hosts that have been added to the hosts configuration file. Now that Nagios is aware of the hosts that we will be monitoring, let's define an example command that could be used to monitor one of the services on the hosts.

Nagios commands

Before service checks can be executed to start checking a service on a host, there must be a command defined that will be referenced by the service check. Let's put these commands in the /etc/nagios/conf.d/nagios_command.cfg file. We are not going to cover all the commands needed to monitor your OpenStack cloud here. Instead, we will cover the concept of a defined command. Each command has a name that will be referenced later and a path to an executable. The executable runs and returns a zero through three return codes. Zero means the check succeeded, one means the check is warning, two means the check failed, and three or another return code indicates the status is unknown. An example of command definitions in the /etc/nagios/conf.d/nagios_command.cfg file looks like this:

```
define command {
command_line /usr/lib64/nagios/plugins/check_nrpe -H $HOSTADDRESS$
-c $ARG1$
command_name check_nrpe
}
define command {
command_line /usr/lib64/nagios/plugins/example_command
command_name example_command
}
```

Note that the commands are executed live in /usr/lib64/nagios/plugins/. If you add executable scripts that Nagios will use to check services, it is good practice to add the executable scripts to this directory. If the intent of example_command was to verify that the host's hostname was set properly, its content may look like this:

```
#!/bin/bash
HOSTNAME=`hostname`
if [ -z $HOSTNAME ] || [ -z $1 ]; then
echo "Host name or argument was blank"
exit 3
fi
if [ $HOSTNAME == $1 ]; then
echo "Hostname is $HOSTNAME"
```

```
exit 0
fi
if [[ $HOSTNAME == *$1* ]]; then
echo "Hostname is $HOSTNAME and contains $1"
exit 1
else
echo "Hostname is not $1"
exit 2
fi
```

Note that there is a case for all four of the possible return values. It is not required that return codes three and one be returned. Unfortunately, this command could be terribly useless. If it were associated to a host, it would never be accurate because it would always execute on the host that Nagios is running on and would never return success for any host other than the host that Nagios is running on. This creates the need for a command to be executed remotely on a host that is being monitored.

The check_nrpe command shown in the nagios_command.cfg file is important as it allows exactly that – remote execution of commands on the hosts being monitored. **Nagios Remote Plugin Executor** (**NRPE**) checks are issued to the hosts via this command definition. Make sure that the NRPE command definition is in the nagios_command.cfg file. On each of the hosts that will have NRPE checks run on them, the NRPE service must be running and TCP port 5666 must be open for the Nagios host to connect to. Make sure this is a private connection. If this is unsecured traffic, it can open a security risk. To ensure the NRPE service is on each of your overcloud nodes, connect to each one and install, enable the service and add the Nagios server, 192.0.2.1 in your example cloud, to the allowed_hosts parameter in the configuration file /etc/nagios/nrpe.cfg:

```
overcloud-node# sudo yum install nrpe -y
overcloud-node# sudo chkconfig nrpe on
overcloud-node# sudo vim /etc/nagios/nrpe.cfg
overcloud-node# sudo systemctl start nrpe
```

The configuration for these checks requires that a host and a command name be passed and that all the details about the command that is run beyond its name will be defined on the remote host that the command is being executed against. These details live in /etc/nagios/nrpe.cfg on each host. At the very bottom of this file, there is an include_dir directive:

include_dir=/etc/nrpe.d/

However, for this example, we will put the commands right in the `nrpe.cfg` file underneath the `include_dir` directive. By configuring the NRPE commands, Nagios is able to connect to the nodes and execute the commands to carry out the monitoring. Let's use the `example_command` script as an example NRPE command and make it a useful definition. On the control node, put this line in the `nrpe.cfg` file:

```
command[check_hostname]=/usr/lib64/nagios/plugins/example_command control
```

If this configuration is added to each of the overcloud nodes with the respective hostnames and the `example_command` script is installed at the referenced location, then it could be used to verify that a hostname was properly set on each of the OpenStack nodes.

There is a large collection of commands and NRPE commands that need to be defined on the Nagios host and the hosts that Nagios is monitoring. Look at the example code included with this book for the executable scripts, commands, and NRPE definitions needed to execute the service checks that will be referenced in the rest of this chapter.

Now that a basic overview of adding hosts, commands, and service definitions of Nagios has been covered, let's take a look at the kinds of checks that are useful to monitor the health of an OpenStack cluster.

Monitoring methods

As you begin to design availability monitoring for your cloud, there are at least three schools of thought on the kinds of checks that should be executed. These should be mixed and matched as you deem appropriate to establish the coverage you need to monitor the services in your OpenStack cluster. You may also come across other methods of designing health checks that can be mixed with what is discussed in this chapter.

The first type of check is the service status check. This type of check runs a simple Linux service status check on each of the services. If the service status script returns successfully that the service is running, the health check is successful. The problem with relying on these is that many OpenStack services have the ability to automatically heal from a loss of communication with each other. You can run a service check on an OpenStack service that is up and running but is actively attempting to reconnect to the database or to the message bus. OpenStack is intelligent enough to know when these kinds of connections have been severed and will attempt to re-establish the connections. In this case, the service status check will return positive but users will not be able to use the cluster because things are not functioning properly.

Then come the API checks. This type of check will call the APIs, making sure that a simple resource list returns successfully. This type of check makes service checks a bit redundant if you only have one instance of each service. If the service check fails, the API check will fail too, and there is no need to have two checks telling you that something is not working. The API check can do the job just fine and provides a more thorough check.

API checks become insufficient once you have multiple instances of a service running. In this case, a combination of service checks and the API checks is necessary. If a service is being load-balanced, the API check is important to make sure that the instances are being load-balanced properly. However, if one of the services gets hung for some reason, the API check will start to flap or change from a successful state to a failed state and back to a successful state over and over as the load-balancer still sees both services but one is not healthy. To better monitor this situation, adding extra checks that monitor each instance of the service is necessary. You will have to use your best judgment to decide whether the right way to monitor each individually is to use service checks or API checks.

The third and final check type we will discuss is the resource creation check. These checks use the APIs to actually create resources and then verify that they were successfully created in the cloud as expected. We will not get a chance to look at these. An example of this would be a check that creates an instance and adds it to a network to ensure that it can be connected to. This kind of health check is a little bit more complex to design but is more comprehensive in its coverage.

A word of caution when using this type of check: there are rows that are created in a database for each of these resources and their associated counterparts that are created.

In some cases, when resources are deleted, the rows are not deleted from the database, the resource is just labeled as having been deleted, and the database row remains. A very obvious example of this is a Nova instance. All the instances that are ever launched have a row in the database that can be used to construct a historical record of instances that have existed. Be careful not to bloat your database with health checks and degrade the service with excessive database records unrelated to your end users. There are certain scripts included with OpenStack that are intended to archive some of these records from resources that have been created and deleted. As of now, I've not had them function as expected. There is also discussion in the community to add more archival tools to help manage this kind of archival. Archival generally will just move the records from the tables that active resources are using into an identically structured table with a different name in the same database; they are not completely deleted.

Now that we have taken a look at some of the concepts used to help in defining configurations in Nagios and the kinds of checks that are useful to monitor your OpenStack cluster, let's start to add some checks to start to establish health status beyond the hosts being up or not.

Non-OpenStack service checks

We are not going to cover generic non-OpenStack service checks in depth here. There is plenty of information you can search for on the Internet that can guide you on generic service checks. We will put these and the OpenStack service checks into `/etc/nagios/conf.d/nagios_service.cfg`. For OpenStack, it is important to at least add a host load and a disk usage check for each host. OpenStack can consume an excessive amount of disk space and processor load, and the whole cluster can become cranky very quickly if either is used beyond one of the hosts' capacity. There are many other generic checks that can and maybe should be added to your OpenStack hosts, though you will have to research others and choose the checks that you deem advantageous. Here are examples of the configurations for checking the load and disk space on `/var`:

```
define service {
check_command check_nrpe!load5
host_name control
normal_check_interval 5
service_description 5 minute load average
use generic-service
}
define service {
check_command check_nrpe!df_var
host_name control
service_description Percent disk space used on /var
use generic-service
}
```

These checks should be set up for all your hosts. You can see that the disk space check uses the default check interval and the load check is set up with a custom check interval. Also, it is important to note that both of these checks are done over NRPE. This means that the Nagios host connects to the NRPE service on the specified hosts, and the command is executed local to the host being monitored. To see the commands executed for these checks, look at the Nagios commands that are included with the code with this book. Now let's get into some OpenStack-specific availability checks.

Monitoring control services

The control tier of an OpenStack cloud has the most moving parts that will need to be monitored. There are a few services that need at least a basic service connection validation. They include, but are not limited to, MySQL, RabbitMQ, and MongoDB. More monitoring can certainly be added beyond simple connection checks to monitor connections, queue sizes, and other statistics of the services. For now, we'll just add a connection check to make sure that these services are running:

```
define service {
check_command check_mysql!nagios! nagios_password
host_name control
service_description MySQL Health check
use generic-service
}
define service {
check_command check_nrpe!check_rabbitmq_aliveness
host_name control
service_description RabbitMQ service check
use generic-service
}
define service {
check_command check_nrpe!check_mongod_connect
host_name control
service_description MongoDB service check
use generic-service
}
```

You can get the scripts for Rabbit and Mongo from `https://github.com/mzupan/nagios-plugin-mongodb` and `https://github.com/jamesc/nagios-plugins-rabbitmq`.

Next, we get into checking OpenStack services. We are going to add API checks to make sure that the service is running and that it is not in an error state. Packstack includes a few scripts to cover most of the API services. A few are additional to Packstack. Let's add the service stanzas for Nagios for the API calls:

```
define service {
check_command keystone-user-list
host_name control
normal_check_interval 5
service_description number of keystone users
use generic-service
}
define service {
check_command neutron-net-list
```

```
host_name network
service_description Neutron Server service check
use generic-service
}
define service {
check_command nova-list
host_name control
normal_check_interval 5
service_description number of nova instances
use generic-service
}
define service {
check_command glance-index
host_name control
normal_check_interval 5
service_description number of glance images
use generic-service
}
define service {
check_command cinder-list
host_name control
normal_check_interval 5
service_description number of cinder volumes
use generic-service
}
define service {
check_command heat-stack-list
host_name control
normal_check_interval 5
service_description number of heat stacks for admin
use generic-service
}
define service {
check_command ceilometer-resource-list
host_name control
normal_check_interval 5
service_description number of ceilometer resources
use generic-service
}
define service {
check_command swift-list
host_name control
normal_check_interval 5
service_description number of swift containers for admin
use generic-service
}
```

With these basic checks in place, a set of successful checks in Nagios will show that services are up and running and the API services are healthy enough to list the resources that are being managed. There is a collection of services on the control node that are not API services. It is usually enough to do a service status check on them to make sure they are running. Let's add a service status check for the rest of the services that are not API endpoint services. You will want to add configuration stanzas that look like this for each service:

```
define service {
check_command check_nrpe!check_service_name
host_name 10.100.0.4
service_description Service Name service check
use generic-service
}
```

Do that for each of the following services, replacing service_name and Service Name with the actual service names:

```
openstack-ceilometer-alarm-evaluator
openstack-ceilometer-alarm-notifier
openstack-ceilometer-central
openstack-ceilometer-collector
openstack-ceilometer-notification
openstack-cinder-backup
openstack-cinder-scheduler
openstack-cinder-volume
openstack-glance-registry
openstack-heat-api-cfn
openstack-heat-engine
openstack-nova-cert
openstack-nova-conductor
openstack-nova-consoleauth
openstack-nova-novncproxy
openstack-nova-scheduler
```

Remember that each of these services points to a corresponding NRPE command, so the hosts that these services run on will have to have the corresponding NRPE command defined on them.

Monitoring network services

Next, let's take a look at monitoring networking services. Networking services in general usually stay running, and things that go wrong are happening inside the running service. We will go ahead and put a service status check on each of them and add additional checks to make sure things are working across the board. Start with giving each of the network services a service status check – the same checks that the control services got:

```
neutron-dhcp-agent
neutron-l3-agent
neutron-lbaas-agent
neutron-metadata-agent
neutron-metering-agent
neutron-openvswitch-agent
neutron-ovs-cleanup
openvswitch
```

Now, let's look at what can be monitored to make sure that when these services say that they are running, the network service is actually running. The configuration we have used in this book uses VXLAN tunnels to build overlay networks for OpenStack tenants. What this means is that each compute node is connected to the network node and to each other with VXLAN tunnels that encapsulate the traffic so that the network that actually connects the nodes doesn't directly handle the network traffic within Open vSwitch. When a packet is put on the network by an instance, it is tagged with a local VLAN to the compute node. When the packet moves from the compute node to the tunnel between that compute node and either another compute node or the network node, it gets retagged and the encapsulation header is added to the packet. This header somewhat hides the VLAN tag given to the packet to move across the tunnel from the actual network that connects the nodes that the packet is moving between. After the packet reaches the destination node it was sent to, the header is removed, and the packet is then retagged again to move around locally within this next node. These tunnels are handled by a running OVS process, and the ports and interfaces that are added and removed are handed by the running neutron OVS agent running on each node. Here is where, just because an agent is running, it does not mean that traffic is flowing from node to node without issue. To monitor that traffic is actually flowing, we can build our networking resources in OpenStack that mock the process followed when an instance is attached. Instead of attaching an instance to it, we will expose an interface to the node that we want to make sure is properly networking and send a ping across it. If the ping succeeds across the interface exposed to the node, then we know that the entire encapsulation just described is working properly.

The first step to set up the networking is to create a network specifically to do the tunnel monitoring on. Make sure you have sourced your admin's `keystonerc` file, and create the network. Refer to *Chapter 2, Identity Management,* if you need to revisit the `keystonerc` file. Here's the command that is being discussed:

```
control# neutron net-create tun-mon
control# neutron subnet-create tun-mon 10.0.0.0/24
```

Take note of the network ID from the `net-create` command; you will need that at the end of this process. Next, manually create a neutron port for each node that you want to monitor tunnel connectivity on. This is most likely each of your compute nodes. You don't need to do this for the network node or the control nodes. The control node has nothing to do with your networking in OpenStack, and the network node is the node that you will be pinging to verify tunnel connectivity. Here's the command that is being discussed:

```
control# neutron port-create --name moncompute --binding:host_id=compute
$NETWORK_ID
```

`NETWORK_ID` is the ID of the network that was just created. You should be able to use `grep` to port out of a neutron port list now:

```
control# neutron port-list | grep moncompute
```

This will include a port ID, a MAC address, and an IP address. You will need those for the final step. Finally add a port in the OVS on the target machine and give it an IP address.

```
compute# ovs-vsctl -- --may-exist add-port br-int moncompute \
-- set Interface moncompute type=internal \
-- set Interface moncompute external-ids:iface-status=active \
-- set Interface moncompute external-ids:attached-mac=${PORT_MAC} \
-- set Interface moncompute external-ids:iface-id=${PORT_ID}
compute$ ip link set dev moncompute address ${PORT_MAC}
compute$ ip a add ${PORT_IP}/24 dev moncompute
```

Now, on the compute node, you can verify that all is in place. First, look at the interface:

```
compute# ip a s moncompute
```

You should see an interface that has the IP address and MAC address that corresponds to the Neutron port you created for the node. Next, look at the routing table:

```
compute# ip r
```

You should see a routing entry for the subnet that you gave to the `tun-mon` network. In the example command earlier, it was given as `10.0.0.0/24`, so the routing entry should look like the following line of code:

```
compute# 10.0.0.0/24 dev moncompute proto kernel scope link src
${PORT_IP}
```

Finally, on the compute node, you can look at the port in the OVS:

```
compute# ovs-vsctl show
```

Look for a port named `moncompute`. It will have an interface named `moncompute`, which is the interface you just looked at, and it will have a VLAN tag number. The last thing to do is get the DHCP address from the network you created and ping it. To get the DHCP agent's IP address, show the interfaces in the network namespace for your network on the network node:

```
control# ip netns exec qdhcp-${NETWORK_ID} ip a
```

You will see `127.0.0.1` and another address, probably `10.0.0.2` or `10.0.0.3` if you used the same subnet as the example. This address is the DHCP agent for the network you created. Now, try and ping that address from the compute node:

```
compute# ping 10.0.0.3 -c 3
```

If you get a reply ping when you do this, your tunnel is working. The way this traffic is funneled over the wire ensures that the VXLAN tunnels in your OpenStack cluster are working properly. These resources should stay in place unless you delete them but the OVS interface on the compute node will have to be recreated if the node is rebooted. You will have to get creative about how to persist or re-establish the interface if the node is rebooted. The ping can be added to Nagios so that you get your tunnel status with the rest of your checks. Let's move on to compute services and take care of the ping there.

Monitoring compute services

The final set of services to monitor are those on the compute node. Here, you can make sure a couple of services are running and add the ping from the section you just finished. Start with the generic service status check for these services:

```
neutron-openvswitch-agent
openvswitch
neutron-ovs-cleanup
openstack-ceilometer-compute
openstack-nova-compute
```

Then add a service configuration to Nagios that will run the ping command to check your tunnel connectivity:

```
define service {
check_command check_nrpe!check_ovs_tunnel
host_name compute
service_description OVS tunnel connectivity
use generic-service
}
```

As you can see, this is just an NRPE check command that will execute a ping from the compute node to the network node.

Summary

As a final word of caution, remember that successful health checks across a cluster do not equate to a positive end user experience. Make sure to be in communication with end users about their experience, and use the cluster for your own purposes to ensure you are familiar with the experience the end user is receiving.

In this chapter, we have gone through a list of items that should be checked to monitor the health of an OpenStack cluster; this list is not exhaustive though. The best practice is to keep an eye out for possible points of failure and add checks that make sure that something that could potentially degrade services is monitored for its health.

The last topic for us to cover is troubleshooting. When these health checks start to alert, how should you go about diagnosing the problem and resolving the issue? In the last chapter, we will take a look at how to troubleshoot each of OpenStack's components.

13
Troubleshooting

With the number of moving parts that make up an OpenStack installation, it is inevitable that as the cluster is brought up for the first time, a few things will not work. Further, as the cluster operates, there will also be service failures that should be addressed. It is very important to be able to troubleshoot a running OpenStack installation. Let's take a look at some of the details of how things work under the hood and how to figure out what is going wrong when things are not working properly. We will look at general troubleshooting and then take a look in detail at a few components to help troubleshoot each of them.

The OpenStack debug command-line option

Most of the OpenStack command-line commands support passing --debug before a subcommand. For example, with hypervisor or server lists, it could look like this:

```
$ openstack --debug hypervisor list
$ openstack --debug server list
```

Note that --debug is put before the subcommand being executed. Using the debug option like this is helpful because it will show curl commands for each of the API calls that are being made from the command-line client to the API endpoints. Hosts and ports are included in this, so if your command-line client has trouble connecting to the endpoint, you can use the debug option to get more detail. If you need to see what information is being sent from or returned to the command line, the debug option will show those details.

Tailing the server logs

There is an extensive collection of logs across an OpenStack cluster, and they are your best friend. Often a good place to start when an API call succeeds but the end result is not as you expect is to tail the log files of a component that you're having trouble with. You can do this as, or right after, you execute the command that you are seeing failure with. For example, if you are having trouble connecting to Keystone, it might not be running properly or might be throwing errors for some reason. Start a tail on `/var/log/keystone/keystone.log` and rerun the command that is failing. This is shown in the following command:

```
$ tail -fn0 /var/log/keystone/keystone.log
```

In this command, `-f` indicates that we follow the log or show new entries as they are added. The `-n0` means show the most recent zero lines; in other words, any previous content in the file is suppressed so that you only see new entries when you run the command. All of the OpenStack components are going to have logs in `/var/log/{component_name}/` except Swift-proxy, which will be in `/var/log/messages`. Horizon will have extra logs in Apache's log files at `/var/log/httpd/*log`.

As another example, if Nova is not launching an instance properly, there could be a problem with the API collecting enough information or a problem with the scheduler finding a place to put the running instance. Sometimes, it is helpful to tail all the logs in the log directory instead of just one. Tailing more than one log will get you output from all the services that are related to a component. This is shown in the following command:

```
$ tail -fn0 /var/log/nova/*.log
```

Notice here that `*.log` is indicated and not an asterisk. This is because if `logrotate` is rotating logs, there could be `.gz` files that you do not want to tail because they are binary. The tail's initial output will indicate what file a new entry is coming from, which will help you narrow down the service that needs a little help.

Often, the case is that one component is showing an error in its log, but the error is being generated by another component, and the error that you are trying to debug was a result of a call being made from one component to another. To debug this kind of behavior, it is helpful to know how components interact with each other. In the following sections, let's take a look at the major components in OpenStack for you to get a better idea of how they interact with each other so that you can effectively debug them.

Troubleshooting Keystone and authentication

Nothing is more frustrating than not being able to log in to your cluster to see what is going on. Thankfully, OpenStack offers an authentication override to bypass authentication and allow you to make Keystone calls to see services, endpoints, and other Keystone resources. This is called using the Keystone admin service token. In *Chapter 2, Identity Management,* we looked at creating a keystonerc file. To use this service token to override authentication, you need to use a similar methodology.

 If you encounter trouble using your admin token to override authentication, check the file /usr/share/keystone/keystone-dist-paste.ini and look in the sections [pipeline:public_api], [pipeline:admin_api], and [pipeline:api_v3] for admin_token_auth. If the key admin_token_auth is missing then this method of authentication has been disabled.

Start by getting the current service token value from the keystone.conf file:

```
$ grep admin_token /etc/keystone/keystone.conf
```

The value that Keystone's admin_token is set to can be passed with a service endpoint URL to Keystone and authentication will be overridden. To keep it separate from your original overcloudrc file, create a new file with a name such as overcloudrc_token. Get the OS_AUTH_URL environment variable from overcloudrc and populate the new file with the following content:

```
export OS_AUTH_TYPE=token_endpoint
export OS_TOKEN={value of keystone.conf admin_token }
export OS_URL=http://{auth_url_ip}:35357/v2.0/
```

It is important to note here that OS_URL uses the IP address from the OS_AUTH_URL variable and uses the Keystone administrative endpoint on port 35357 and not the public or internal endpoint on port 5000. Port 5000 is for authenticated traffic, and port 35357 is for non-public administrative traffic, such as service token calls to override authentication. It is not recommended that port 35357 be publicly accessible. Next, source this file so that the environment includes these variables:

```
$ source overcloudrc_token
```

Now, run an `openstack` command such as `hypervisor list` or `endpoint list`. The first thing you want to do here is reset the admin user's password and then stop using these service tokens. It is very bad practice to operate on Keystone using the service token. So, first, update the admin user's password. Then, unset the token environment variables and set the `AUTH_TYPE` back to `password`. The following command shows this:

```
$ openstack user set --password supersecret admin
$ unset OS_TOKEN
$ unset OS_URL
$ export OS_AUTH_TYPE=password
```

Make sure you unset both `SERVICE` environment variables. If Keystone sees `OS_SERVICE_TOKEN` and not `OS_SERVICE_ENDPOINT`, it will complain. If it sees `OS_SERVICE_ENDPOINT` and not `OS_SERVICE_TOKEN`, weird things happen.

Once you have unset the service token environment variables, make sure that you update the password in your `overcloudrc` file and re-source it. If you do not source it, then the new password will not be used. This is shown in the following command:

```
$ source ~/overcloudrc
```

If you want to see the value that is being used of any of the variables that you have sourced, then just use the `echo` command; for example, to see your password that is being used, execute the following command:

```
$ echo $OS_PASSWORD
```

If you have other problems to troubleshoot, start with the Keystone log file at `/var/log/keystone.conf`. From there, you will need to move on to verifying the endpoints by listing them with endpoint list and making sure that they are correct and that they point to running services. If you are having authentication issues from the services, you need to make sure that the password in the configuration file for the services matches what is in Keystone's database. You can simply use the `user set` command for the service users to force Keystone's password for the service users to match what is in their configuration file. The username to use should be indicated in the service's configuration file right next to the password it is using.

Troubleshooting Glance image management

It's not often that Glance needs troubleshooting. There are two common ways that you will have things fail related to Glance:

- If Glance cannot access the filesystem that it will be writing to when it is saving an image into the registry
- If Nova cannot get an image that has been assigned to launch an instance with

In the event that you are not able to save an image to the registry, you will just have to read the logs in /var/log/glance/*. Depending on the backing store that you have chosen, or that has been configured for you, there will be different errors. In most cases, when you resolve these errors, you will have a working Glance service.

When a new instance is launched on a compute node, one of the things that the Nova compute service does is to check whether it has a cached copy of the image that the instance is being launched from on the compute node. If it does, it will use the local cache; if it does not, it will connect to Glance and download a copy of the image to its cache and then continue launching the image. This, again, is a case where you will have to watch the logs and read the errors that are being thrown. Follow the logs and verify connectivity from the compute node to the Glance endpoint. This should help if nova-compute cannot get images from Glance for the instances it is launching.

Troubleshooting Neutron networking

Neutron is a bit of a special case among the OpenStack components because it relies on and manages a fairly intricate collection of transport resources. These may be created as a result of Neutron resources being defined by end users. There is not always a straightforward correlation at first sight. Let's walk through the traffic flow for an instance to make sure that you know which agent is doing what within the Neutron infrastructure.

The first thing that an end user will do before launching an instance is create a network specific to their tenant for their instances to attach to. At the system level, this translates into a network namespace being created on the node that is running the Neutron DHCP agent. Network namespaces are virtual network spaces that are isolated from the host-level networking. This is how Neutron is able to do isolated networks per tenant. They all get their own network namespace. You can list the network namespaces on any Linux host that has network namespaces enabled, using the `ip utils` command:

```
$ ip netns
```

When you run this command, if you have some networks already defined, you see namespaces named qdhcp-{network-id}.

 The letter Q is a legacy naming convention from the original name Neutron had, which started with the letter Q. The old name had a legal conflict, and it had to be changed.

So a `qdhcp` network namespace is a namespace created to house the DHCP instance for a private network in Neutron. The namespaces can be interacted with and managed by the same tools as the host's networking by just indicating the namespace that you want to execute commands in. For example, let's list the interfaces and routes on the host and then in a network namespace. Start with the host you're on. The following command shows this:

```
$ ip a
$ ip r
```

The interfaces listed should be familiar, and the routes should match the networks you are communicating with. These are the interfaces and routes that the host that OpenStack is installed on is using. Next, get the ID of the network you would like to debug, and list the interfaces and routes in the namespace using the `netns exec` command. This is shown by the following command:

```
$ ip netns exec qdhcp-{network-id} ip a
$ ip netns exec qdhcp-{network-id} ip r
```

The same commands are executed inside the namespace and the results are different. You should see the loopback device, the DHCP agent's interface, and the routes that match the subnet you created for your network. Any other command can also be executed in just the same manner. Get the IP address of an instance of the tenant network and ping it:

```
$ ip netns exec qdhcp-{network-id} ping {host-ip-address}
```

There is even an independent `iptables` rule space in this namespace:

```
$ ip netns exec qdhcp-{network-id} iptables -nL
```

The ping is important because by pinging the instance that is running on the compute node from the `qdhcp` network namespace, you are passing traffic over the OVS tunnel from the network node to the compute node. OpenStack can appear to be completely functional – instances launch and get assigned IP addresses – but then the tunnels that carry the tenant traffic aren't operating correctly, and the instances are unreachable by way of their floating IP addresses.

To debug an unreachable host, you have to traverse more than one namespace. The `qdhcp` namespace we just looked at is one of the namespaces that an instance needs to communicate with the outside world; the other is the `qrouter`. The OpenStack router that the instance is connected to is represented by a namespace, and the namespace is named `qrouter-{router-id}`. If you look at the interfaces in the `qrouter`, you will see an interface with the IP address that was assigned to the router when the tenant network was added to the router. You will also see the floating IP added to an interface in the `qrouter`.

What we are working towards is tracing the traffic from the Internet through the OpenStack infrastructure to the instance. By knowing this path, you can `ping` and `tcpdump` to figure out what in the infrastructure is not wired correctly. Before we trace this, let's look at one more command:

```
$ ovs-vsctl show
```

This command will list the bridges and ports that Open vSwitch has configured in it. There are a couple of them that are important for you to know about. Think of a bridge in OVS as somewhat analogous to a physical switch, and a port in OVS is just a network port on a switch or a physical port on a physical switch. So `br-int`, `br-tun`, `br-ex`, and any others that are listed are virtual switches and each of them has ports. Looking at `br-int` first, we can figure out that this is the name of the bridge that all local traffic will be connected to. Next, `br-tun` is the bridge that will have the tunnel ports on. Not all hosts will need to use `br-ex`; this is the bridge that should be connected to a physical interface on the host to allow external traffic to reach OVS. Finally, only in the case of a VLAN setup is there a custom bridge setup. We are not going to look at them in this book, but you should know that the three we are discussing are not the exclusive list of OVS bridges that OpenStack uses. The last thing to note here is that some of these bridges have ports to each other. This is just like connecting two physical switches to each other.

Now, let's map out the path that a packet will take to get from the Internet to a running instance. The packet will be sent to the floating IP from somewhere on the Internet. It should go through the physical interface, which should be a port on `br-ex`. The floating IP will have an interface on `br-ex`. The virtual router will have an interface on `br-ex` and `br-int` and will have iptables rules to forward traffic from the floating IP address to the private IP address of the instance. For the packet to get from the router to the instance, it will travel over `br-int` to `br-tun`, which are patched to each other, over the VXLAN tunnel to `br-tun` on the compute node, which is patched with `br-int` on the compute node that has the instance's virtual interface attached to it.

With this many different hoops to jump through, there are quite a few places for traffic to get lost. The main entry points for debugging start with namespaces. Start by trying to ping the instance or the DHCP server for the tenant in the namespaces and move to tcpdump if you need to. Pings and tcpdumps can be a quick diagnosis of where traffic is not flowing. Try these tests to track down where things are failing:

- Make sure that ICMP is allowed for all IP addresses in the security groups
- Ping the instance from the `qdhcp` namespace
- Ping the instance from the `qrouter` namespace
- Tcpdump ICMP traffic on physical interfaces, `br-int`, `br-tun`, and `br-ex` as needed

These pings establish first that traffic is flowing over the VXLAN tunnels and that the instance has successfully used DHCP. Secondly, they establish that the router's namespace was correctly attached to the `qdhcp` namespace. If the ping from `qdhcp` doesn't succeed, use `ovs-vsctl show` to verify that the tunnels have been created and check the Open vSwitch and Open vSwitch agent logs on the network and compute node if they haven't. If the tunnels are there and you can't ping the instance, then you need to troubleshoot DHCP. Check `/var/log/messages` for DHCP messages from the instance on the network node, and boot an instance you can log in from the console to try to `dhclient` from the instance if you don't see messages from the instance in the logs.

If the initial pings don't succeed, you can use `tcpdump` on the Open vSwitch bridges to dig a bit deeper. You can specify which interface you want to listen on using the `-i` switch on `tcpdump`, and you can drill down to where traffic is failing to flow by attaching to the Open vSwitch bridges one at a time to watch your traffic flow. Search the Internet for `tcpdump` and `ping` if you are not familiar with using `tcpdump`:

```
$ tcpdump -i br-int
```

Start with `br-int` on the compute node, and make sure you see the DHCP traffic coming out of the instance onto `br-int`. If you do not see that traffic, then the instance might not even be trying to use DHCP. Log in to the instance through the console and verify that it has an interface and that `dhclient` is attempting to contact the DHCP server. Next, use `tcpdump` on `br-int` on the network node. If you do not see the DHCP traffic on the network's `br-int`, then you may need to attach to `br-tun` on the compute and network nodes to see whether your traffic is making it to and across the VXLAN tunnels. This should help you make sure that the instance can use DHCP, and if it can, then traffic should be flowing properly into the instance from the network node.

Next, you may need to troubleshoot traffic getting from the outside world to the network node. Use `tcpdump` on `br-ex` to make sure you see the pings coming from the Internet into the network node. If you see the traffic on `br-ex`, then you will want to check the `iptables` rules in the `qrouter` namespace to make sure that there are forwarding rules that associate the floating IP with the instance. The following command shows this:

```
$ ip netns exec qrouter-{router-id} iptables -t nat -L
```

In this list of `iptables` rules, look for the floating IP and the instance's IP address. If you need to, you can use `tcpdump` in the namespace as well, though it is uncommon to do this. Look up the interface the floating IP is on, and attach to it to listen to the traffic on it:

```
$ ip netns exec qrouter-{router-id} ip a
$ ip netns exec qrouter-{router-id} tcpdump -i {fip-interface}
```

Using this collection of tests, you should be able to identify where the trouble is. From there, check logs for Open vSwitch and the Neutron Open vSwitch agent for tunneling, the Neutron Open vSwitch agent and Neutron DHCP agent for DHCP issues, and the Neutron L3 agent for floating IP issues.

Troubleshooting Nova launching instances

Nova has good logging and will most likely have a pretty good error message to indicate what is going wrong if you have trouble getting instances to launch. You would want to check logs for `nova-api`, `nova-conductor`, and `nova-scheduler` on the control tier, and on each compute node where there is a `nova-compute` service running. Let's look at what each of these agents does so that you know where to look when something is going wrong.

When a Nova command is executed, it talks to the `nova-api` service. If an error is received directly when a Nova command is executed, this is generally where you can find more detail beyond the immediate error message returned.

Once a command to act on an instance is accepted into the Nova infrastructure, there are two services that handle passing actions to the compute nodes – `nova-scheduler` and `nova-conductor`. `Nova-scheduler` is just what its name suggests. It handles the decision-making as to where to schedule resources across the collection of compute nodes that are available. Start with the scheduler's log file if instances are falling into an error state quickly. There is a chance that there are criteria mismatches for the instance to launch. If the scheduler suggests there are no available compute nodes, then use the nova `hypervisor list` command to see a list of available compute nodes:

```
$ openstack hypervisor list
```

This will show all the Nova services and their statuses. The services of the `nova-compute` type are the nodes that the scheduler will need to have an *up* status to be able to schedule resources properly.

Once the scheduler has made a decision about where to launch an instance, it will pass on the information to `nova-conductor`. The main purpose of `nova-conductor` is to remove the need for the compute nodes to access the database. There is communication between `nova-conductor` and the `nova-compute` service on each of the compute nodes via the message bus and they access the database on their behalf. If your instances are having trouble spawning, then they have been scheduled, and there is most likely an issue with nova-conductor or its communication with the nova-compute nodes. Check the logs in `/var/log/nova` for `nova-conductor` and the assigned compute node's `nova-compute` service.

Troubleshooting post-boot metadata

Images are built and added to Glance as generic reusable images. This means that there isn't any data included to launch the image that is built into it. To provide the image with configurations to allow login and customization, the images should include a service called cloud-init. Cloud-init calls back into OpenStack to get SSH pub keys and post-boot configuration commands. There is a predetermined URL that cloud-init calls into: `http://169.254.169.254`. If you are getting an access-denied error when you try and SSH to your floating IP address, it is probably because cloud-init is failing to get the SSH pub key for your authorized keys file, you are using the wrong username, or you are using a prepackaged image that you have downloaded with a username other than root.

To troubleshoot the metadata service, make sure that you have an image that you can connect to the console. CirrOS is a good option for debugging things like this; just remember not to use CirrOS for anything other than testing and debugging. CirrOS is an insecure distribution of Linux and is intended only for testing and debugging. Once you have logged into the console of an instance, use `curl` to mock the call that cloud-init will make:

```
$ curl http://169.254.169.254/latest/meta-data/
```

You will have to memorize the IP address that is used or search the Internet, but you can make a call directly to the IP, and it will give you a list of paths that can be used. Try making a call to the metadata service in this order:

```
$ curl http://169.254.169.254/
```

```
$ curl http://169.254.169.254/latest/
```

```
$ curl http://169.254.169.254/latest/meta-data/
```

You can see that in the second call, the latest is listed, and in the third call, metadata is listed. In the third call, there is a further collection of paths that can be called to get different information. If you have gotten this far, then the metadata service is working, and maybe cloud-init is not installed on the image that you are having trouble accessing. When you call these URLs and you get errors, you will have to check logs in two places to figure out what the issue is. The first one is the Neutron metadata proxy service. Look in `/var/log/neutron` and you will see one log named `metadata-agent.log` and other logs named `neutron-ns-metadata-proxy-{network-id}.log`. To troubleshoot the metadata service that is not working, you just need to look at the `metadata-agent.log` file. Make sure there aren't any errors in it. There are only a few configuration options in this file. If you get any connection error in the logs, check the URL and port for the Nova metadata proxy service. If you get an authentication error, check that the shared secret matches the shared secret value in the `nova.conf` file on the control tier.

If your investigation takes you up to Nova, you will need to look at the API service. The Nova metadata service is a subprocess of `nova-api`. Check the logs of `nova-api` and check the errors that are there. Configuration options related to `nova-api` are in `nova.conf`.

When troubleshooting the metadata service calls, the issues are usually closer to the instance itself, such as cloud-init not being installed, the instance not using DHCP properly, or in early cases of setting up the cluster, the neutron-metadata-agent not being configured properly to proxy calls.

Troubleshooting console access

The URL for console access is generated from a property that is set on each compute node. Look at the `nova.conf` file on one of your compute nodes for the `novncproxy_base_url` property:

```
novncproxy_base_url=http://control.example.com:6080/vnc_auto.html
```

This base URL is the address of the `nova-novncproxy` service that will be able to create a console connection to the instance. In the web interface, this URL is retrieved for you when you select the console tab for an instance. At the command line, you can use Nova's `get-vnc-console` and pass the `novnc` type to get the console URL:

```
$ nova console url show --novnc {instance-id}
```

This will return a URL that will include `base_url` from the compute node the instance is running on and an authentication token to access the console with. If you paste this URL into a web browser, there are a few steps that happen under the hood to connect you to the instance's console.

First, you need to be able to connect to `nova-novncproxy`. This runs by default on port `6080` on the control tier. Once the request to connect to the instance's console is established, the token that is passed in the URL is passed to `nova-consoleauth` and validated in `nova-cert`. If all that succeeds, then the connection to the instance on the compute is established and the console is provided through the web browser.

If you are having trouble with console connections, make sure that the base URL is pointing to the `nova-novncproxy` service, and that you can connect to the `nova-novncproxy` service. If you see a console window, but the console is not being displayed, then you need to check that `nova-consoleauth` and `nova-cert` are running and check the logs for errors in validating the token. If there aren't any errors in validating the token, check the `nova-novncproxy` log to ensure that a connection to the instance can be made.

Troubleshooting Cinder block storage

Troubleshooting Cinder is similar to troubleshooting Glance. The issues that arise are dependent on the backing storage that you use. The best course of action to troubleshoot it is to watch the logs in `/var/log/cinder/*` and correct errors that show up in there. These logs are where you will find errors related to creating Cinder volumes and connecting them to the instances.

Troubleshooting Swift object storage

The trick to troubleshooting Swift is to remember that it has a proxy tier and a storage backend tier. The proxy is essentially the API layer to Swift, and it is the place to start looking for errors in Swift. As mentioned earlier, Swift-proxy does not have its own log file. Its logs will show up in /var/log/messages. If things look good in the proxy's logs, then take a look at the storage backend, and see whether there are any errors in the Swift storage logs.

Troubleshooting Ceilometer Telemetry

Ceilometer has a large number of dependencies and agents that run across the cluster to collect data on the resources being used. Once again, to troubleshoot this component, the best course of action to take is to watch the logs. Any errors that you see should be resolved to ensure that telemetry data is being collected.

Troubleshooting Heat orchestration

Heat is one of the widest-reaching components within the OpenStack infrastructure to troubleshoot. This is because each template that is built is different and has different dependencies among resources created in the stack that is launched. Further, it is able to depend on or create almost any resource within OpenStack. As with the other components, the best starting place is with the Heat logs in /var/log/heat. This will give you a good indication of where things might not be going correctly.

If a stack is launched and does not successfully complete, but you do not see any errors in the Heat logs, then the issue may be in the instances. Heat has callbacks from the running instances that must work for the orchestration of data and the ordering of instance creation within a stack.

If you review the section in this chapter on the metadata server, you will notice that the post-boot configuration that is run on an instance is delivered by the metadata service. When cloud-init fires and receives post-boot configuration, it will log what it is doing in /var/log/cloud-init.log. There are callbacks into Heat that are included in your cloud-init scripts that must alert Heat that it is time for the next instance in a stack to be created if it is dependent on a previous instance in the stack completing its provisioning. The service that is called back into is the heat-cfn service. If you see failures calling back into the heat-cfn service, you will need to get this URL and verify and troubleshoot this connectivity.

Getting more help

It is not possible to foresee every error or troubleshooting scenario that could happen in an OpenStack installation. If you need further help in debugging and installation, start with `http://ask.openstack.org`. Each of the projects that we have covered in this book also has a community of developers that actively work on it. You can connect with them through mailing lists, forums, IRC channels, and bug trackers. To find contact information for each of these communication channels, start with `http://www.openstack.org`. If you do not find what you are looking for there, then search the Internet to get further information for each of the projects.

Summary

In this chapter, we have taken a look at some of the architecture and workflow of a few of the components of OpenStack. Knowing how the components operate will help you to troubleshoot issues when they arise in your OpenStack cluster. With the number of modules that are present in OpenStack, you have to follow the order of operations that are being run, validate their success, and check for errors as you go along.

Having looked at troubleshooting OpenStack, we have come to the end of this book. The information in this book is core to OpenStack and defines many of the basic concepts and methodologies that are baked into the OpenStack project. The project moves quickly, and new features are added very rapidly, but because the information here is central to a base installation of OpenStack, you should be able to reference the majority of this book for many releases to come from the OpenStack project.

Index

D

dashboard
about 2
endpoints 27
data
graphing 95-97
database 129
data store 91
Docker image
importing, to Glance 119
Docker instance
launching 120
Domain Name System (DNS)
name server 42

E

external network access
about 47
external network, creating 50
network, preparing 47-49

F

Fedora qcow cloud image
reference 30

G

Generic Routing Encapsulation (GRE)
about 39
ways, of accomodation 39, 40
Glance 4
Glance configuration
about 119
Docker image, importing to 119
Glance image management
troubleshooting 151
Glance image registry 29

H

HAProxy 126
Heat
about 8
for autoscaling instances 104

Heat orchestration
troubleshooting 159
Heat Orchestration Template format
about 101
reference 101
high availability 127, 128
Horizon 2

I

identity management
about 19
Keystone, interacting with in
dashboard 24-27
services and endpoints 19
image management
about 29
Glance image registry 29
image, building 33-35
image, downloading 30, 31
image, registering 30, 31
web interface, using 31, 32
instance management
about 57
flavors, managing 57
floating IP addresses, managing 61
instance, communicating with 63
instance, launching 60
instance launching,
web interface used 64-70
key pairs, managing 58, 59
security groups, managing 62
instances
autoscaling, with Heat 104
Internet Control Message Protocol (ICMP) 6

K

Keystone
about 2, 3
troubleshooting 149

L

lb_server.yaml type
reference 111
Load Balancer as a Service (LBaaS)
about 104

R

RDO
  installing, Packstack used 10
  installing, Triple-O used 11-14
ring files
  about 88
  creating 89, 90

S

scripts, for Mongo
  reference 139
scripts, for Rabbit
  reference 139
Secure Shell (SSH) host key 4
server logs
  tailing 148
services and endpoints
  about 19, 20
  new user, logging in with 23
  project, creating 22
  projects 21
  role, granting 23
  roles 21
  user, creating 22
  users 21
Software Defined Networking (SDN) 5
stack
  launching 101-104
Swift 7
Swift cluster
  architecture 84
Swift object storage
  troubleshooting 159

T

telemetry 91
templates, for autoscaling example
  reference 104
Triple-O
  used, for installing RDO 11-14

troubleshooting
  about 147
  Ceilometer telemetry 159
  Cinder block storage 158
  console access 158
  Glance image management 151
  Heat orchestration 159
  Keystone and authentication 149, 150
  Neutron networking 151-155
  Nova launching instances 155, 156
  post-boot metadata 156, 157
  Swift object storage 159

U

User Datagram Protocol (UDP) 40

V

virt-install 5
Virtual IPs (VIPs) 128
Virtual Local Area Network (VLAN) 39
VXLAN tunnels 40

W

web interface
  about 113-115
  object file management 85-87
  using 31, 32
web interface external network setup 51-55
web interface management 42-46